JAMES WHITCOMB RILEY
HOOSIER POET

Books by Jeannette Covert Nolan

NOVELS

SECOND BEST

NEW DAYS, NEW WAYS

MYSTERIES

WHERE SECRECY BEGINS

PROFILE IN GILT

JUVENILE BOOKS

THE YOUNG DOUGLAS

BARRY BARTON'S MYSTERY

RED HUGH OF IRELAND

HOBNAILED BOOTS

THE GAY POET

(The Story of Eugene Field)

CLARA BARTON OF THE RED CROSS

JAMES WHITCOMB RILEY

(Hoosier Poet)

JUVENILE SERIALS

MYSTERY AT CRAYCROFT

(St. Nicholas)

THE VERY EXCLUSIVE SALAMANDERS

(The Portal)

There never were such stories as those told by "Orphant Annie"!

James Whitcomb Riley

HOOSIER POET

By

JEANNETTE COVERT NOLAN

Illustrated by ROBERT S. ROBISON

NEW YORK

Julian Messner, Inc.

PUBLISHED BY JULIAN MESSNER, INC.

8 WEST 40TH STREET, NEW YORK

Fourth Printing, August 1946.

PRINTED IN THE UNITED STATES OF AMERICA

BY MONTAUK BOOK MANUFACTURING CO., INC., NEW YORK

Foreword

AS A NATIVE of Indiana and a resident of Indianapolis, I have written with Hoosier pride and affection this account of the life of James Whitcomb Riley, endeavoring to portray him fairly and at full-length. The sources upon which I have drawn for information have been not only his own works, the few biographical sketches of him, the articles to be found in magazines, periodicals and the files of old newspapers, but also conversations and correspondence with many persons who knew him and were his friends.

The question, often debated, of whether he possessed true genius or even an exceptional talent, has been no concern of mine in these pages. That while he lived he was rated as a genius is not to be doubted. Fame and honor were his in unstinting measure and if, as has been said, he was merely the product of an era, to the critical standards of that era he was more than satisfying.

But whatever the ultimate verdict, whether or not his poetry will survive and he is to be accorded a niche among American immortals, his reputation among the people who loved him is secure and will go unchallenged.

In Greenfield on the Court House square stands his statue, erected with the voluntary offerings of pennies from the nation's schoolchildren. A little way down the street is his homestead, the property now of the James Whitcomb Riley Old Home Society, restored, visited each year by throngs of pilgrims.

In Indianapolis there are the magnificent hilltop mausoleum in Crown Hill cemetery; the Lockerbie Street house; the James Whitcomb Riley public school. In the east wall of the Indianapolis Public Library, cut deep into the limestone, is an inscription: *"This door opens on land given to the people of Indianapolis by James Whitcomb Riley,"* and just inside the door, off the corridor, is the spacious Riley Room where scores of boys and girls flock every day for hours of reading and story-telling. At the front entrance of the same beautiful building are gates with a bronze tablet:

> THESE GATES ARE THE GIFT
> OF THE
> CHILDREN OF INDIANAPOLIS
> IN LOVING REMEMBRANCE
> OF THEIR FRIEND
> JAMES WHITCOMB RILEY

Foreword

Most constant, perhaps, and most poignant of all reminders is the James Whitcomb Riley Hospital for Children, a unit of the Indiana University Medical Center in Indianapolis. The hospital, fostered by the James Whitcomb Riley Memorial Association, was dedicated on Riley's birthday, October 7, 1924. As fine and modern, as completely equipped as any in the United States, superbly staffed by trained surgeons, specialists and nurses, this institution annually relieves the sufferings of thousands of crippled children.

In the city and the state where his memory will ever be as a living presence, the James Whitcomb Riley Hospital is a monument of ministry rather than of mourning, the perfect tribute to the Hoosier Poet.

JEANNETTE COVERT NOLAN

Indianapolis, February, 1941

Acknowledgments

FOR INFORMATION or assistance in research, or for both, I wish to thank the following persons:

From Greenfield, Indiana: Mr. and Mrs. Dale Spencer and Mr. Richard Spencer, Mrs. Leah K. Early, Mr. Arthur Downing, and Mr. William A. Hough.

From Indianapolis: Mr. Luther L. Dickerson, Librarian; Miss Carrie E. Scott, Miss Evelyn Sickels, Mrs. Charles M. Wells, Miss Mary Cain, Miss Mary Fishback, Miss Miriam Atkinson, Miss Lois Zimmerman and Mrs. Hortense Kelly, all of the staff of the Indianapolis Public Library; Mr. and Mrs. Paul Shideler and Mrs. Florence Webster Long, of the staff of the Indianapolis *News;* Mrs. Harriet Eitel Johnson, Mr. George C. Hitt, Mrs. Meredith Nicholson, Jr., and Mrs. John W. Cravens.

I would also acknowledge a special debt of gratitude to my good friends, Mr. and Mrs. J. Gordon Sherer and Mr. B. Howard Caughran, for invaluable advice, encouragement, and help.

Selections from Riley's Poems
by courtesy of Bobbs Merrill Company, Indianapolis

Illustrations

Introduction

*I*T IS a pleasure to commend this story of the life of James Whitcomb Riley, not only for its recital of the steps by which he rose to fame, but for the fidelity with which he is pictured in his environment. He won every right to be called the Hoosier Poet, for no other Indianian in any literary form has so faithfully as Riley recorded the social aspects of his time—the simplicity, the homeliness, the humor and pathos of a people still in the pioneering stage when Riley began, all-consciously, to observe their ways and their manners. Riley got from books all that was necessary for him to know; and, of even greater value in his education, what his discerning eyes and his attentive ears gathered from the folk of simple mind and heart in his own community.

I salute Mrs. Nolan for the vivid picture she gives of

Riley's boyhood and early manhood, which could not have been treated so effectively in a formal biography. And there is much of cheer in the story of Riley as a sign-painter, or as providing entertainment for the crowds that collected about an itinerant doctor.

Riley's career followed obviously an inevitable course, and he appeared, with characteristic modesty, at the gates of song just as the West and South were beginning to be recognized as potential sources of the stuff of real literature. Mark Twain and Bret Harte were laying the foundations of their fame and Joel Chandler Harris was calling attention to the richness of Negro life—a field which in fiction, drama and melody, even today, seems inexhaustible.

Speculation is idle as to what would have been the effect on Riley of a formal education. The speech of the little-schooled Hoosier of the countryside was to him more important than Latin and Greek would have been. He was destined to become his own Horace and Theocritus!

In the years when Riley's verse, timidly launched from Greenfield, began to catch the eye of exchange editors in newspaper offices beyond Indiana's borders, there was such a thing as a distinctively American humor. It was finding expression largely through journals identified with the name of some writer. Perhaps in the last years of the nineteenth century we laughed more easily than we do now; but at any rate there were Bill Nye and Bailey, the *Danbury News* man, and the merry men of Texas *Siftings,* and "M. Quad" of a special weekly edition of the *Detroit Free Press,* Robert J. Burdette of the *Burlington Hawkeye,* and Eugene Field, whose varied talents were displayed first in Denver, but more importantly after he had transferred his portfolio to Chicago. And from Chicago the world began to hear a little later from George Ade, one of the most loyal of Hoosiers, who was to discover in American college life new material for drama. Riley's humorous verse and sketches no doubt helped gain for him readers of his poems in which a tender, sincere pathos was the dominant note.

The benignant powers that had Riley in their keeping moved him to Indianapolis at a time when there were many understanding persons among the citizenry, ready to give him encouragement. Mrs. Nolan has most happily presented the town as it was when the young poet became visible in and about the *Journal* office. In addition to those named in this book as friends of Riley in those days, I would mention Miss Anna Nicholas, a woman of keen literary discernment, long of the staff of that paper, and the stimulating friend of many Hoosier aspirants; and at the *News* office, Riley had in Dan L. Paine a sympathetic and intelligent critic, to whom he was devoted until Paine, himself the author of a small but admirable sheaf of poems, passed on.

I speak carefully when I say that one could find in Indianapolis at that time some person who could answer a question in almost any branch of knowledge; and in this group Riley found warm welcome and appreciation. He, too, was a man of rare knowledge. Once he had discovered his vocation Riley let nothing interfere with it. He meddled with nothing that could disturb his tranquillity as the predestined interpreter of the life of his own people and their setting. Political contests in Indiana were always tinged with bitterness, but to Riley the battles for supremacy were wholly mystifying. I once asked him if he had ever voted. He answered that on one occasion he had tried to vote for a friend who was a candidate for a county office. But, he said, he was sure he had marked his ballot improperly, and thereafter he had refrained from voting!

Riley had a sense of his own dignity and I could give instances of his annoyance in being accosted familiarly by individuals who were merely casual acquaintances. He disliked anyone's slapping him on the back, or touching him—"manhandling" him, as he called it. Toward the end of his life, the automobile was a great resource to him and I was often his companion on journeys into the country. Frequently, after a long silence, he would say: "What a beautiful world this is and what a lot of grand people there are in it."

That was Riley, the gentle, kindly man and the poet of the people, whose writings bring to a large constituency the sweetness and charm of his own spirit.

MEREDITH NICHOLSON

"Our own Riley is the one distinguished son of Indiana whose life and works are the very essence of the Hoosier State." ... GEORGE ADE

"More than any American poet Riley will live as the people's poet." ... HENRY WATTERSON

"Everybody who read Riley loved him, and those who met him loved him even more. He never disappointed you; he was the man of his works. He was simple, affectionate, truehearted; and his humor was the ground quality of his personality." ...
WILLIAM LYON PHELPS

JAMES WHITCOMB RILEY

HOOSIER POET

Chapter One

SMALL BOY sat on the stoop of the substantial white-painted frame house fronting Greenfield's Main Street. Spring sunshine slanted warmly upon him, gilding his hair to pale fluff like the silken down of a dandelion ball, flushing his freckled cheeks. In one hand he grasped a pencil and a sheet of paper, sticky and crumpled, lined with his own scrawled sketchings; the other held a piece of bread and jelly at which he occasionally nibbled. His eyes, blue as the April sky, were fixed on the highway.

The year was 1853; the street a segment of the National Pike, chief artery of commerce across an expanding continent. In Maryland and Pennsylvania, even in neighboring Ohio, the Pike was old, no longer a source of excitement to those people who lived beside it. Here in Indiana the Pike had been only recently constructed. Broad and straight as a knife blade, surfaced with planks, it slashed through fertile flat country which less than forty years ago had been unbroken forest, the hunting grounds of Delaware and Miami tribes. Dwellers in Indiana villages bordering the Pike had not yet ceased to marvel at the tide of pilgrims constantly pressing westward: home-steaders, whose destination was government land in Kansas and Oklahoma; sturdy peasant families, freshly emigrated from Europe, plodding toward Illinois, the Mississippi and obscure distances defying the imagination; hopeful seekers after sudden wealth in the California Gold Rush; adventurers, vagrants, tramps.

This morning the covered wagon trains had to contend with an eastbound traffic. A circus had been playing in Indianapolis, the state capital twenty miles away, had pulled up stakes and set out for the cities of Ohio. The circus was routed through Greenfield; since dawn the immense vans had been lumbering and creaking past, to claim young Bud Riley's attention, to fascinate him. From his vantage on the stoop, he had seen such sights!—darling shaggy ponies; cages of curiously colored, chattering birds; mysteriously cloaked vehicles that must surely contain every variety of jungle beast; dozens of monkeys with skinny, beckoning paws and contorted visages like tiny masks of comedy. Unless luck failed him, Bud believed he might finally see a clown. Patiently, alertly, he

4

watched (a clown, any minute now!) until the door opened behind him and a voice hailed.

"Hi, Bud?"

"Hi, Johnty." He glanced back. His brother was emerging from the house.

"What on earth you doing out here?"

"Just sittin'."

"You've been in that spot for hours. Are you glued?"

"I don't *think* so." Bud wriggled experimentally. "No."

"Don't you know Father wants you?" John was eight, big for his age, sandy-complexioned, rather severe of countenance. He felt a sense of responsibility for Bud, five years his junior. "Father's made something."

"Has he?" Bud's tone was casual. The simple statement that Father had made something was not in itself astonishing, for Father could make *anything*. His fingers were deft and skillful, his inventiveness unlimited. Though a lawyer by profession, and a successful one, many trades were at Father's command. Why, he was even a doctor, of sorts, concocting medicines from herbs; queer aromatic draughts that had the power to cure stomachache and other ailments . . . Bud shrugged, his gaze reverted to the street, the jolting wagons.

"Listen," John said. "It's a surprise. For *you.*"

"Oh." This, of course, was different. A surprise? For him? But Bud was cautious. "Not medicine, Johnty? Not a tonic?"

"No, a real present. Go on in, Bud, and get it."

5

Silently Bud weighed the possibilities—Father's present against the prospect of seeing the clown, who hadn't come and perhaps might never come. Deciding in favor of Father, he threw the bread and jelly into the grass, stuffed pencil and paper into the pocket of his overalls and got to his feet.

At the door he paused. "Johnty, if there's a clown—"

"I'll call you."

"I *love* clowns."

"Did y'ever see one?"

"No," said Bud. "Except in pictures."

As he entered the house, Mother was just descending the curved stairs, her hand lightly sweeping the banister, her face a smiling, gentle oval, framed by wings of smooth dark hair. In the lower hall she stopped and surveyed Bud.

"My dear boy, how soiled you are! I must clean you up."

"Not now," Bud said briskly. "I'm in a hurry. Father—"

"I know. He's waiting in the kitchen. But you'll have to be washed a *little* bit."

Seizing his sleeve, Mother led him into a bedroom. She poured water from a China pitcher into a flower-decorated basin on the toilet stand. With sponge and soap she scoured at jelly stains and accumulated dust.

"There!" she said, rubbing him dry, kissing him. "You're ready."

6

"Ready for what, Mother?"

"Didn't Johnty tell you?"

"He said Father's made me a present."

"A lovely one." She nodded. "And after he has given it to you, he's going to take you downtown."

Instantly Bud was apprehensive. He was very shy; and while it must be deemed an honor to be taken downtown by Father, such excursions usually meant encounters with strangers to whom Bud would be introduced and have to speak politely. Father was a popular and important man in the community; he had been the county prosecutor, a member of the state legislature; he had scores of friends to waylay him at every corner of the Square, eager to discuss politics with him, elections, business. When Father became engrossed in these discussions, he was likely to forget completely the bored child dragging at his coat-tails.

Once, on a similar outing, Bud had slipped off unnoticed and bolted for home. It was an escape, but one he would not try again, for Father had been angry. And Father's temper was a thing to be avoided.

"You won't mind, dear?"

He would mind, awfully.

"But you'll be brave, for my sake?"

"All right." He flung his arms around Mother's slender shoulders as she knelt beside him; he burrowed his nose in the ruffles of her bodice. For her sake he would have braved the perils of the universe.

7

When they went into the kitchen, Father was at the ironing board; and Bud stifled an impulse to giggle, for Father, erect and spare, bearded and dignified, had an apron tied about his waist. An apron!

"Well, son?" Father himself was laughing, his black eyes snapping under their arched brows. Extraordinarily gay, he lifted Bud to the table. "A slight token of my affection." He whisked something from the ironing board; he bowed. "With my compliments, sir."

It was a suit of clothes, beautiful and entire: long pants, a fitted vest with a red back and a buckle, a diminutive coat with a notched velveteen collar, each garment exactly Bud's size yet perfectly tailored in the height of adult fashion.

Bud couldn't think of a single word to say. He had never guessed that sewing was another accomplishment at which Father was expert. He balanced proudly as Father dressed him in the dazzling new things; and when he had hopped down once more, he strutted around the room and then out to the stoop to let John admire him.

"I'm going downtown," he announced. "To court, with Father." He was quite reconciled to that now. "Bet you wish you had a suit like this Johnty."

"A monkey suit," said John patronizingly. "You look like one of those monkeys."

"I do not!" Bud had stared at his reflection in the mirror; he knew how he looked. Like a man! When Father came out of the house, Bud ran to him. "Goodbye, Mother. Goodbye, Johnty."

At Father's heels, he hastened to the street, ignoring the circus vans still heavily trundling over the planks. He had seen the best of the procession, anyway—and probably the clown would never have appeared.

Chapter Two

PERHAPS MR. RILEY, strolling that morning with his son, considered the changes which he had seen in Greenfield since 1844, when he had brought his bride here. Then the village had only fourteen years of existence behind it and was a settlement of scattered log houses, with puncheon floors and oil-paper windows. Mr. Riley had built just such a home for himself, a cabin, equipped with furniture which he made with his own capable hands from the abundant timber of the maple and beech grooves. To distinguish it from the others, he tacked a shingle to his door, above the latch-string. *Reuben A. Riley* was printed on the shingle.

Soon afterward he further advertised his coming. In the *Greenfield Reveille*, Hancock County's first newspaper, he stated that he was an attorney at law, with "Office at my residence."

Those were the crude and difficult days of the Middle West, when the wilderness crowded about the sparse clearings, bears and panthers stalked the nearby forests; at night wolves howled and the owl hooted. Abruptly, with the cutting of the National Pike through Indiana, the pioneer conditions had been altered. In 1850 Greenfield was incorporated as a town. Now it could boast of sixty dwellings and a population of three hundred. Its improvements had been many and rapid: the draining and filling of the pond which marred the contours of the public square and the construction of stores and shops on this redeemed property; the springing up of sawmills, gristmills and taverns; the establishing of a terminal for the Indiana Central railway which next year would be finished. The feeling of growth and progress was in the air. The old courthouse had been abandoned as too small for modern usage, a new one would replace it. Plans were afoot to grade the streets, to gravel or pave the sidewalks, to restrict the roaming at large of dogs, pigs and cattle.

As the village had grown, so in proportion had Mr. Reuben Riley prospered and assumed a prominent part in its affairs. Clients came down the National Road in increasing numbers, through the toll gates, to employ the services of the attorney at law. Fees were plentiful and solid; gathering them in, he determined to provide more comfortable lodgings for his family, his pretty young wife

11

and two sons. Perhaps there would be more children. Anticipating the future, Mr. Riley moved the log cabin to the rear of the lot and built the fine new frame house in its stead.

From their first month in Greenfield, the Rileys won friends and were recognized as people of character. Though this was a "backwoods" district, the village had its share of cultured folk. Among them, Elizabeth Marine Riley was reputed to be something of a poet; she frequently contributed verses to the local papers. As a sensitive, intelligent woman, she was esteemed almost as much as for her qualities of devoted wife and mother and hospitable hostess. Greenfield loved her, and she sincerely returned its genuine affection. If, in the beginning, she had sometimes been lonely for her native Randolph County, she had long ago realized that she was never going back, that henceforth this was to be her home, her town . . .

During the intervals "between courthouses," as a wag had put it, the sessions of the circuit court were held in temporary quarters. It was to the Methodist Church on South Street that Mr. Riley and Bud went today.

As Bud had expected, there were strangers about, many of them, farmers who had hitched their teams to the fence outside the church, villagers lounging on the steps and in the vestibule. Father, pausing to chat with everyone, was besieged by questions: Would the state vote Democratic in the 1854 election? Did Mr. Riley think that private schools were better than the free education which the state of Indiana had guaranteed its citizens with the adoption in 1816 of the constitution? And what about this agitation among Indianapolis clubwomen for equal suffrage? Wasn't that a newfangled, outlandish notion? A man came forward to assert heartily: "If you stump the county in the next campaign, I aim to be on deck, Mr. Riley. I haven't forgot your speaking when you campaigned for Polk. I've heard fire an' brimstone, hell-an'-Mariar orators before; but, by jacks, you've got 'em all beat!"

To each query and to the tribute to his eloquence, Father replied gravely and cordially. At last, with Bud following, he strode into the church and up the middle aisle to the bench. There he halted and, eyes twinkling, he said in a loud voice:

"Your honor, I've brought the court a visitor." He pushed Bud forward. "This, sir, is Judge Riley."

"You don't say!" The frock-coated, bespectacled gentleman on the platform (which was, of course, the pulpit on Sundays) leaned to peer at the little boy before him. "Well, glad to meet you. And what's the rest of your name, Judge Riley?"

Bud gulped back his embarrassment. "My whole name," he murmured, very red, conscious of an audience, "is James Whitcomb Riley."

13

"You don't say!" The august gentleman on the platform seemed pleased and amused. "You know, do you, whom you were named for?"

"For the Governor of Indiana."

"You don't say! When were you born, Judge Riley?"

"On October 7, 1849."

"And you're going to practice at this bar? To be a lawyer, like your Dad?"

Bud looked uncertainly at Father, and then nodded. "Yes, I want to be a lawyer."

The gentleman chuckled. "You don't—"

"—*say!* cried Bud, explosively, and with such precise imitation that a gust of laughter swept over the big room.

Only Father was frowning; and as he ushered his son to a pew and seated him, he commented: "I know you have talents as a mimic, Bud. Yet there are times when you must restrain yourself. That was the judge—"

"You told him *I* was the judge."

"I was just joking."

"Is he mad because I talked like him? Are you mad, Father?"

"No. But you must be careful of your manners. . . . Now you sit here quiet as a mouse and listen. If you really want to be a lawyer—"

Bud was quiet; he listened mutely; and it was not long before he was positive that he did *not* want to be a lawyer. Indeed, he could think of nothing worse! Assembled about the bench, Father and the others were deep in legal

14

argument which seemed to have no end, no interruption except when huge books were produced, when there were dull and interminable readings. To Bud, who could not understand a word of it, the language of the law books was senseless. He was tired; his legs were numb in the tight pants, the vest cramped his chest, the buckle dug into his spine. Through the window he could see the sun climbing higher and higher. He wished that he had stayed on the stoop, in his good old dirty overalls! His head sank against the stiff wooden back of the pew; after a while his eyes closed. . . .

"Bud, it's noon." Father was shaking him softly. "The court is recessing. Wake up!"

He straightened with a jerk. "I wasn't asleep. Can we go home?"

"I can't," Father said. "I've work to do. But if you could manage to go alone—"

"I could! I can, Father!" He slid down. His feet felt funny, prickling as if pins had been stuck in them, his knees wobbled. But he was so happy to be released!

"You behaved nicely." Father patted his shoulder. "Here's a reward."

"A penny!"

"I suppose I should advise you to save it. But if I were you, I'd spend it."

"Yes. Yes, sir. Thank you, sir." He was careful of his manners!

Fast as his short legs would carry him, he dashed up the

15

street, toward the square and the general store on the corner. He knew what he would buy. Last week, marketing with Mother and Johnty, he had spied a treasure in the showcase. He went into the store, pointed a stubby forefinger and said breathlessly: "Please, ma'am, sell me that."

The clerk, a young woman in a calico frock, looked over the counter at the customer. "That book?"

"Yes, ma'am. I've got the money." He displayed the coin in his moist palm.

"You have a penny, and the book is marked twenty-five cents." She took it from the showcase, a little volume in a neat leather binding. " 'Francis Quarles' *Divine Emblems*,' " she read from the title page. "You don't want this."

"It's a poetry book."

"Yes. But what would you do with it? And it's too expensive." She smiled coaxingly at him. "Pick out something else for your penny. Rock candy? Licorice? Cinnamon drops?"

He shook his head. A tear welled on his lashes.

The clerk was troubled. "Aren't you the little Riley boy?"

"Yes, ma'am."

She hesitated. The book was not new; nobody ever had wished to buy it before; and the boy seemed so very sad at the refusal. "I hardly knew you in those clothes," she said.

16

"My father made 'em."

"They're grand. . . . I guess I could put the other twenty-four cents on your father's monthly bill. His credit is good. Shall I wrap up the book?"

"No, ma'am." He could not risk that; she might change her mind. He tossed his penny on the counter, clutched the book and trotted out.

He walked for a block and then ran again, for up ahead he saw someone, as wonderful a person as there was in the world.

"Hey!" Bud shouted. "Hey!"

It was Martin Riley, Father's brother—and, by some peculiar circumstance which Bud never could fathom, not a man like Father, but a boy, though a big boy, tall and gangling and awkward. He lived in Indianapolis where he was a printer; but he came to Greenfield often, to stay with Mr. Reuben Riley's family.

"Well!" Uncle Mart wheeled, grabbed Bud and swung him off his feet in a mighty hug. "Well, hello!"

"I been to court." Bud had a great deal to say and plunged immediately into confidences. "This is my new suit that Father sewed. I acted like the judge, the real one, an' they laughed, an' Father told me to be still as a mouse. I saw the circus, too, ponies an' everything. But I'm not going to be a lawyer!"

"I should think not." Uncle Mart grinned. "Not for some time, at least. What's that under your arm?"

"I got me a book. A poetry book."

17

Uncle Mart whistled. *"Divine Emblems,* eh? My lawsy-daisy! . . . Reckon your ma will feed me?"

"Yes, I know she will. Are you hungry, Uncle Mart?"

"I'm always hungry," Uncle Mart said. "Let's hustle, skeezics."

Hand in hand, they hustled.

Chapter Three

O AN OBSERVER it might have seemed that
Greenfield was a village swarming with children
and that in summer most of them congregated in
the Riley yard.

Certainly there could have been no better place for play.
Though the plot which edged Main Street was reserved by
Mother for her flowers, lilacs and dahlias and roses in pro-
fusion, all the rest was the boy's domain.

It was a shady playground. Locusts overhung the house;
willows trailed branches like the fluttering curtains of a
tent. Maples and elms stood in irregular rows, with here
and there a giant horse chestnut, its beautiful shiny buck-
eyes hidden in rough-skinned burrs, waiting for the early
autumn when they would drop to earth and lie like bits

19

of polished mahogany in the grass. Behind the house was the small orchard, tended and pruned by Uncle Mart: the cherry tree which in May burst forth in a feathery mass of miraculously white bloom and later was studded with luscious fruit as red as rubies; the pear tree with boughs that sheltered the two dome-shaped beehives; the apple trees so precious that each seemed to have its distinctive personality. In one apple tree (the "Prince's Harvest") Uncle Mart had built a playhouse, with a ladder up the trunk by which it could be reached. He said that this leafy retreat was intended only for John and Bud, but he himself often climbed to it and read novels or scribbled rhymes or the beginnings of stories he never quite finished.

Between the orchard and the stable was a grape arbor, checkered inside by the sun through the lattice and the knotty vines. Currant bushes and a stunted quince tree fringed the arbor; at its end was the stable where Old Sorrel lived, munching his hay and oats, switching his tail at the flies invading his stall.

Once Old Sorrel had been a giddy colt, and then a spirited steed to draw Mr. Riley's stylish red-trimmed rig. Now he was content to be saddled by the boys and jog lazily around the yard or down the road, half a mile and back.

"I keep the horse because I'm so fond of him," Mr. Riley was wont to say. "Sell Sorrel? I'd as soon think of selling a relative!"

20

Hoosier Poet

Had Bud been asked, he might have said that of all the attractions on the premises, he most enjoyed the wood-house. Much was to be seen and examined there. Its floor space had been partitioned into two separate rooms. In the first were the logs and kindling, primly stacked and giving off a delicious odor of pine bark and sawdust. The second room was a workshop, with Father's tools arranged on low shelves: compass and brace-and-bit, hammers, screw-drivers and scrolls, and a magical hand plane which turned out curly loops of satiny shavings. Here also were the cane poles and other fishing tackle, with a net fes-tooned above them.

The workshop was so definitely masculine in most as-pects that Father was inclined to regret Mother's finding it necessary to store any of her paraphernalia there. "My dear," he would remark fretfully, "your quilting frames, the soap kettles and the kraut-shredder—they strike a discordant note."

In this opinion Bud concurred, though silently; and Mother always smiled. Nevertheless, her things remained. Without her express orders, no one would have dreamed of banishing them.

Just outside the back door of the woodhouse was Bud's own private kingdom, a rectangle of stubbly earth which he had used for numerous purposes and now had con-verted into a mud-pie bakery. He was thinking earnestly of being a baker when he was a man. Some of the tarts coming from his brick oven were, he believed, the equal

21

of anything in the windows of the bakery downtown—at least as far as appearance was concerned. He took infinite patience with the decoration of his products, making elaborate patterns of leaves and flowers on the pies and icing the cakes with a mixture of starch and water.

These wares he offered to passers-by on the Pike; it grieved him that he had no purchasers. But one morning a bizarre-looking man, a traveler who wore his hair long, his mustache fierce and bristling, and hoops of gold in his ears (a gypsy, Johnty said!), stopped at the Riley fence and paid two cents for a pie from Bud's stock. After that, Bud felt encouraged. He had no faith in Johnty's sophisticated assertion that probably the gypsy would return in the night and steal the Rileys' chickens. Nor did he think that the purchaser had been deceived.

"He knew it wasn't *really* chocolate," Bud said. "He winked. Gypsies are nice. I bet it's fun to be a gypsy!"

Uncle Mart, an experienced cook, declared that he would teach Bud to make pies in the kitchen—good ones, of flour and shortening and tasty filling. Uncle Mart often helped Mother with the meals when, as happened several times a week, Father brought unexpected guests for dinner. "It's just a trick," Uncle Mart said, "you'll learn it."

And Bud did learn. It was a glorious day when, after many disastrous preliminaries, he at length baked an honest-to-goodness custard pie and served it at the table.

"They're *eating* it," he thought incredulously; and then: "They *ate* it."

"A very good dessert," Father pronounced.
"The best," said Mother.
"Umm-mm!" grunted Johnty, licking his lips.
Bud beamed.

Scarcely a mile from Greenfield's public square,
Brandywine Creek pursued its ambling course across the
meadows, through the groves. With the coming of hot
weather the steps of every village lad turned toward
Brandywine. Johnty and his boon companions, older boys
like Noah Bixler and Almon Keefer, went there every
day; but it was not until Bud was five that his mother
would grant him permission to go. Then, somewhat reluctantly she said he might paddle in the shallows. He
would have to be careful.

"Don't venture out where it's deep, dear," she admonished, and added: "Martin has promised to keep an eye
on you."

There were two ways to approach the enchanted territory of the Brandywine. You could trudge along the Pike
—which was interesting because of the caravans to be
glimpsed, the conveyances of every description, from ox-
carts of primitive design to spick-and-span Conestoga
wagons behind six horses in gleaming harness ornamented
with bells. Or, if you preferred, you could angle off and
wind through the vacant lots and the woodland where
the underbrush was thick and thorny and rabbits scurried
at the sound of hastening bare feet. Each way had its ad-

23

vantages; both led to the creek bank—and that, after all, was what mattered.

On that first day at Brandywine, Bud felt like something of an outcast. He was afraid he might be regarded as a nuisance by the regular frequenters, and this would have worried him, for even then he had the wish to be agreeable, to please the people around him. As soon as he had arrived and reconnoitered the area to which Mother's solicitude confined him, he set about constructing a little oven and engaged in some mud-pie work. (This, he thought, would be a branch of his larger industry at home.) He had known immediately that the Brandywine was quite as fine as Johnty and the rest had said it was, the tales of it had not been exaggerated. With its uneven, green-clad brink, its clear clean brown water, its bed of shale and sand and glistening white stones, the Brandy-wine was perfect. Secretly he made up his mind to come here as often as was possible. Sometime, in the future, he would have a shack just in this location. The shack would have locks on the door and, though its owner would entertain parties of friends occasionally, there would be intervals when he could retire to the solitude of the shadowy interior and be alone.

While Uncle Mart watched, Bud waded in the shallows; he slipped (once accidentally and then again, on purpose) and got very wet so that his clothes looked as if he had joined the ranks of the revellers in the swimming-hole.

"Better get out and sun yourself," Uncle Mart said. "I wouldn't want to take you back to your ma in that condition. If I told her you'd only paddled, she likely wouldn't believe me."

Bud clambered obediently up the bank and stretched out in a patch of warm sunlight. He tilted his ragged straw hat over his face and was so still that Martin, convinced his little nephew was dozing, wandered off for a quick swim.

But Bud was wide awake, staring up through a rent in the hat crown at the birds which flashed in the canopies of the beeches, seeing and counting the bluejays and warblers and cardinals, hearing their snatches of song, and the hum of insects in the grass. He heard the voices of Johnty and the big boys as they splashed and dived and shouted. What they said, each word and intonation, he would remember, for he had the faculty for remembering, for being able to repeat, weeks and months afterward, whole conversations to which he had listened. Perhaps he would have liked to dive, too, and feel the water on his naked body, closing over his head. But for the moment he was satisfied to bask—and look and listen, to be included in the morning's sun, and yet withdrawn from it. To give his fancy rein and let it soar at will—he liked that most of all!

After an hour, Martin came and prodded the motionless small figure. "Want to explore with me, Bud?"

"Yes." Bud sat up, his hat fell into his lap. He plucked

25

a stem of crab-grass, pensively chewing and sucking the pith from the sheath which gritted on his tongue. "Explore what? Where?"

"You'll see." Mart was grinning. He had pulled on his shirt and pants, but his hair was damp and his bare legs were moss-stained. "Reckon I can escort you to a place that Johnty and Noey Bixler and Almon never *have* known about. It's far, though. Are you game?"

"Sure," Bud said. "Sure, I'm game." He had no idea what he might see. Bears? Wildcats? But with Uncle Mart beside him, he had no fear.

They circled away from Brandywine and pushed through a field where fennel and burdock and ironweed grew breast-high. They went around a poplar cluster and then down to the creek bank once more and along it. There was a ford to cross and above that a dam had broadened the stream so that it had the semblance of a placid lake. Beyond, the trees were like a regiment of giants standing shoulder to shoulder and the Brandywine, its proper size again, seemed to trickle through a dusky tunnel. Martin and Bud walked into the tunnel, the water flowing over their feet, around their ankles. The air was cool, silence was everywhere. At the mouth of the tunnel on a gravelly ledge was a tiny ramshackle cabin.

"Who—who lives there?" Bud was tense, whispering.

"Some friends of mine. You're going to meet them."

"Oh." He would not have been amazed at anything Uncle Mart said, the place was so eerie. And he would not object to an introduction to anybody so fortunate as to live in such charmed and charming surroundings. These would not be like Father's friends. They might be —fairies?

Uncle Mart went boldly up and pounded at the latched window of the cabin. "Irvin!" he called.

Presently the window was thrust open and a woolly head popped into view, a face almost as black as soot, with eyes like mottled marbles.

"How-do, Mist' Mart."

"You got company, Irvin."

"Tha's fine! I'll tell the ol' woman." The woolly head vanished from the aperture.

Uncle Mart lounged to the miniature veranda and sat down. "You'll like Irvin and his wife, Aunt Jane."

"Are they—" Bud faltered, knowing that Irvin simply couldn't be a fairy. Evidently he was a man, though of some grotesque, alien race. But why was he so black?

"The Hunts are Negroes," Uncle Mart said. "The only ones in the county. Reckon you've never seen a Negro before?"

"No."

"Their skin is dark but underneath they're just the same as everybody else, they're human beings."

Irvin shuffled out of the cabin. Behind him was an enormously fat woman, coffee-colored, in a turban and a billowing skirt. She was smoking a pipe and she had a basket on her arm.

"How-do, Mist' Mart," she said, echoing her husband. She glanced at Bud. "How-do, young sir." She chuckled richly. "You starved? Will you sample some biscuits an' grape juice?"

She extracted a bottle from the basket, two pewter mugs, and a plate of cookies. Uncle Mart accepted the food and drink; and after a moment, Bud took the mug which was handed him. He sipped from it, slowly bit into a cookie.

The colored woman had noticed his hesitance. "Don't be skeered," she urged. "Nothin's goin' to hurt you here. Make yourse'f easy."

Uncle Mart and Irvin were talking about fishing; Irvin said he knew a cove where croppies and sunfish could be snagged from dawn to dewfall—"fas' as you can yank 'em in!"

"With what for bait?" Uncle Mart asked.

"Worms," said Irvin. "Grasshoppers."

Bud swallowed the dregs of his grape juice. Irvin's wife replenished the mug and then sat back, puffing at her pipe, smiling amiably. On the roof a yellowhammer sang a shrill little melody. The scene was one of absolute peace and suddenly Bud knew that he was having a most delightful time.

"How about a story, Irvin?" Uncle Mart said. "Not a devil tale, either. Something Bud would like."

Irvin nodded solemnly and launched into a story.

"Once they was a 'possum, a 'coon, a turtle an' a houn'-dog." . . .

Bud was entranced, disposed to linger for another story; but Uncle Mart had risen. "It's near evening. We must be hikin' or my sister-in-law will scalp me."

The Hunts strolled down to the creek's edge and waved them into the tunneled passage between the trees.

"They were slaves," Uncle Mart said, "owned by a Southern planter. They bought their freedom and came across the Ohio into Indiana. An odd sort of freedom, because they have to be on the lookout for people who might catch 'em and ship 'em over the river again. They don't have many friends. Irvin fishes and ploughs and plants his acre of corn, cultivates his tobacco. They've got a garden. I guess they're right happy."

Bud knew nothing about slaves.

"It's a mighty big subject," Uncle Mart said. "Too big for you to puzzle over. It's made trouble—and will make more."

Sloshing through the creek, Bud thought of how envious Johnty would be that he had merely been swimming today—while Bud had met the Hunts. Negroes? But underneath, these dark-skinned folk were the same as everybody else. He resolved to visit them again. Next time he must hear a devil tale!

Chapter Four

*B*UD COULDN'T HAVE said when or by whom he was taught to read. Perhaps he never was taught at all, but discovered by dint of innate ability and concentration that the individual letters of the alphabet combined together and took on meaning as the names of familiar objects, to express familiar actions.

There were books in Reuben Riley's house, and Mother also borrowed novels from the township library. An early conviction of Bud's was that books were to be cherished and handled delicately. During the winter, with Johnty and all the neighborhood children off at school, Bud was left to his own devices and would sit with a book spread on his knees, laboriously spelling out sentences from the pages, pondering them, until at last some of them, the briefer ones, began to be comprehensible.

It was fun, he thought, to see that every day he could read a little farther than the day before.

Writing was more difficult. He had always had the habit of going about with pencil and paper, sketching, drawing; but it was only after prodigious effort that he achieved legible writing. He was gratified when he finally managed it, because it gave him the feeling of independence.

He liked to set down words in precise groupings—that was how the printing looked in his poetry book, which he had concealed in his room upstairs. And it was very nice if the words jingled. He hoped that when he was older he might compose a rhyme which could be read aloud to the family. Mother had done that, and Uncle Mart. Bud could imagine himself doing it.

The hope was strengthened in the first weeks of February. Valentine Day was coming; Johnty had marked the date on the calendar.

"You send valentines to anybody you 'specially like," said Johnty.

"Where do you get 'em?" Bud liked so many people! —almost everybody, in fact.

"At the stationer's. They're made out of lace-paper and mica. They cost ten pennies, each."

"Oh." Bud had just six pennies; he was saving them to buy a bar of Pear's soap.

"But," said Johnty, "you can *make* pretty good ones at home."

"*Oh!*" said Bud.

He collected scraps of paper, blue and red and white; with Mother's scissors he whacked out hearts and darts, and pasted firmly and with abandon. And then he knew that this wasn't enough. Johnty had said the stationer's valentines had poetry, too. Maybe Mother would write it!—

"I would," she said, "but why not do it yourself, Bud? Try!"

Afterward he believed that Mother hadn't really meant him to try, for the results seemed to amaze her.

"My lands! Verses!" she said, when he laid them in her lap.

"Read 'em."

She read them. "They're not bad."

"They're good, *I* think."

"Yes, they are." She was silent a minute. "I wonder," she said, kissing his cheek. "I do wonder—"

They were in the parlor, just Bud and Mother. The clock on the mantel ticked an intimate, unwearied monologue. The sun threw a brilliant arabesque of orange across the Persian-loom, handwoven carpet, on the melodeon, the table with its vase of wax camellias, the brass-based lamp. The day was mild for February and the front door had been set ajar, letting in the sounds of the road, the rumble of a wagon, the clop-clop of hoofs. The branches of a locust tree scratched at the window pane, somewhere a rooster crowed, a robin trilled abruptly.

"It would be only natural," Mother said.

"What?" he demanded.

"If you should write poetry. I've always had the desire to, though I know my talent is slight. The things of mine that have been printed in the *Reveille*—they're inconsequential. But there *is* a tendency, a trait. Yes, undeniably! My father, your grandfather—"

Bud stood, leaning against her knee, clasped in her arms, as she spoke (more, it seemed, to herself than to him) of the Marines, her family. They had come to America from Wales, she said; in origin they were French Huguenot. In this new country they had settled in Maryland, then in Carolina. In 1825 John Marine had come into Indiana, to the Mississinewa River in Randolph County.

"That was a terribly long and dangerous journey," Mother said. "John Marine was months on the way. When he reached his destination he established a mill site—and then he wrote his autobiography in rhyme! All of it, Bud. A poetic narrative. I was a little girl at the time, but I can remember how he used to write and write. For years I had the manuscript, but later it was destroyed. I'm sorry. I wish I could have shown it to you.

"Our cabin was the only one for miles around; it was perched on a bluff at the river's bend, with white oaks in dense masses on three sides of it. My father thought that he could found a town in that beautiful spot. He made a draft of a town and called it Rockingham, and he advertised the lots in rhymes which were published in the state's first newspapers. But Rockingham never amounted to much. I suppose there's scarcely a trace of it on the bluff now. Perhaps future historians will record it. I hope so."

Mother paused. "My father was a builder of boats, and a teacher and a preacher."

"All?" exclaimed Bud.

"All. He wrote a book on religion; he said that the churches ought to be united in one sect, not forever quarreling among themselves. It was not a popular book. . . . He conducted Methodist camp meetings. He was a splendid speaker, very dramatic. Many of his sermons were in verse. When he got up to preach the congregation would applaud him, as if he were an actor on the stage. I think he might have been an actor if he'd been born in another environment.

"Our home was very small and poor but always thronged with people. My father was respected; his life was full and pleasant. Travelers through the forest would stop with us—and stay, for they knew they were welcome. Once Johnny Appleseed came."

"Johnny Appleseed!"

"You've heard of him? That queer old man who planted the prairies with apple trees? Yes, he was at our cabin when I was a child. He tramped all over this region, driving an ox before him. Slung on the ox's back was a sack of seeds. A hundred times a day, two hundred. Johnny would halt, scoop a hole in the earth and plant

34

a seed. He wanted this Middle West to be covered with lovely, fruit-bearing trees which other generations would enjoy. Now we can look about us and see the results of his diligence.

"Johnny was tattered as a scarecrow, his clothes in shreds. He never carried a gun for he said he had no enemies. He hadn't a home, not anywhere, and didn't want one. He had nothing, yet I've never known a happier person."

Mother smiled. "Well, there were other visitors. In those times of sparsely settled country, people would go long distances for contact with their friends and acquaintances. In Randolph County we had big Fourth of July picnics. That's how I met your father, one Fourth of July. He lived on Stony Creek; he was twenty-four years old— and handsome!"

Mother continued, now about the Rileys. "They had come to Indiana from Pennsylvania. The name is Irish, but the Pennsylvania Rileys had a mingled ancestry; they had emigrated from England and some of them had married into German families.

"I never knew your Grandfather Riley, but I think he must have been a fine man. He reared fourteen children and gave them what education was available; he believed in the advantages of book-learning. After struggles at the beginning, he was rather well-to-do. The Miami Indians were his friends; they trusted him. When the harvest failed, he asked the Miamis to come to his house where

35

he loaded their ponies with corn. He was charitable, feeding the poverty-stricken, aiding anyone less fortunate than himself. When he died, very old, he said: 'I have never intentionally wronged any man. I have tried to do right. I do not fear to die.' . . . It was true, Bud, and a fine thing to say."

Bud stirred. "That was my Grandpa Riley?" He must get it straight.

"Yes, your father's father—and Uncle Mart's. Strangely, there seems to have been the talent for writing somewhere in the Riley heritage, also, for Uncle Mart has it, to a degree. Your father has other brothers; one went down south and is there at present. Your Grandmother Riley still lives in Randolph County. Perhaps she will come to see us sometime."

Bud's thoughts had reverted to the Marines. Once Grandpa Marine had spent the winter in Greenfield. Bud had a vivid memory of him—not as a boat-builder, a vigorous and forceful preacher, a writer of epic poetry. Rather, Bud recalled him as an old, old man, grizzled like a Biblical patriarch, an ancient drowsing at the hearth, toasting his shins, glancing up to say, in the metallic tones of the deafened: " 'Morning! How did you rest last night?" For everyone who entered the room, Grandpa had that cheerful, stereotyped greeting: "How did you rest last night?"—until the phrase became a joke at which Johnty and Bud had mocked and giggled.

"This has been your first lesson in family history, hasn't

36

it?" Mother stroked his hair. "Are you impressed?"

He was, indeed. Never before had he visualized himself as connected with the past. Now it was as if Mother had opened a door through which he saw a chain going back, Marines and Rileys, to countries across the Atlantic Ocean, to an era inconceivable. As Mother talked, he had realized that his grandparents were more than portraits in an album or dodderers at the fireside. They were *people* of flesh and blood; men and women, sturdy, plain and sincere, living out honorable lives in days which were real, though so long ago. And Bud must be worthy of them, for what he thought and did and felt was linked, somehow, with their experiences. . . .

That night he regaled Johnty with an account of Grandpa Marine's prowess as a poet. The boys were in their bedroom, the narrow chamber up under the eaves, with a steeply sloping ceiling and one dormer window. Bud's cot was in the corner nearest the door which led to Mother's room. Johnty's larger bed, with its spool-carved headboard, was in the far corner across the width of pine-plank flooring scantily strewn with rag rugs.

"I like Grandpa Marine awfully much." Bud propped himself on his elbow. "I'm going to be just like him."

"A preacher?" Johnty was undressing, hanging his things on pegs. Beside his bed was the bureau which held the lamp. It was Johnty's privilege to regulate the light and thus end a conversation. "A teacher?"

"No, a poet."

37

"Ho!" scoffed Johnty.

"I could!"

"You think that because you made up the valentine verses. Anybody could do that. *I* could."

"Yes," Bud said, "you could. But not *anybody*. That's it, Johnty."

"What?"

"Poetry is in our heads." He watched as his brother donned a flannel nightgown and tossed back the counterpane. "Mother says it's natural with us. . . . Don't put out the lamp *yet!*"

"Have to."

"Please!"

"It's eight o'clock." Johnty turned the wick until it sputtered; he climbed into bed. "Bud, you've got fool notions like all kids. Father wouldn't want you to be a poet. He even fusses about Uncle Mart's pottering with writing. Father says you must be a lawyer, and he knows best. You'll have to earn money when you're a man."

"Will you earn money?"

"Yes." Johnty yawned. "Gosh, I'm sleepy. Good night."

"Is the door to the rafter-room shut?"

"Um-hmm."

"*Is* it?" The low door of that black cavern was just at the foot of Bud's bed. Luggage and other seldom needed articles were kept in there. And perhaps— "Johnty," Bud said, "do you ever hear swishings and swashings in the rafter-room?"

38

Hoosier Poet

"Swishings? No. You mean a rat?"

"Or, something. A ghost, a goblin."

"Oh, hush! Don't be so silly, Bud. Shall I tell Mother to take you in with her again?"

The threat had its effect; Bud hushed. It was only this winter that he had been promoted from the trundle-bed in Mother's chamber to the coveted cot of his own. But long after his brother had lapsed into a gentle snoring, he snuggled wakeful beneath the comforters, his hand touching the poetry book under his pillow.

He didn't know when he went to sleep.

the points of interest they passed. He had an immense pride in his native state. "This is the center of our country," he said, "and the best section of it. Indiana's the greatest state in the Union; and I hope you boys will have the sense to see that and remain here, close to your roots, instead of traipsing off to distant parts. In Indiana we have everything a man could wish for, rivers and lakes, hills and valleys, fertile soil for agriculture, flourishing cities.

"And the people are the best on earth. The average Hoosier is a blend of southern and Yankee stock, with a dash of other nationalities—for some of those wagon trains haven't gone on west; many European immigrants, German, Dutch, French, Scotch-Irish, have stopped midway in the journey and decided to stake a claim. The Hoosier is a combination of several elements, all mellowed down to just the right consistency. He's friendly and cordial, an optimist and not suspicious; but he's shrewd, he's got his feet on the ground and he isn't easily outwitted. He'll make a bargain and abide by it—and see that the other fellows abide by it, as well. He may be isolated but he knows what's going on in the world, and will argue and cuss and discuss till the cows come home! Politics and public questions, they're the Hoosier's meat. At the drop of a hat, he'll tell you all about them. He's stubborn in his views, and conservative; old fashioned, maybe, and slow to be convinced.

"But," said Father, with something oratorical in his manner, "the Hoosier's chief characteristic is his loyalty

42

to his own. He's sentimental there. He may get pretty far away from Indiana at times, but he never forgets it; he never really deserts his kith and kin, his neighbors and old cronies."

Father brandished his whip and flicked at the snow-weighted bough of a poplar by the roadside. "You're average Hoosiers, you boys, John and James Whitcomb Riley —or you ought to be, for you're born and bred. You remember what I'm saying now. My advice is that you stick to the Indiana home-folks, and you can depend on their sticking to you!"

Bud had been listening attentively. "Why are we called *Hoosiers*, Father?"

Mr. Riley laughed. "There are half a dozen explanations, son. You can have your choice. One is that the word used to be a southern planter's term for 'hayseeds' or 'jays.' But I think another is more probable, that the pioneers in this locality had a way of bellowing out *'Who's thar?'* when strangers knocked on their log-house doors at night. 'Who's thar?' If you say that over and over, it gradually sounds like 'Hoosier,' doesn't it? The people in the little towns and on the farms, in the backwoods districts do have a dialect, some of them. They talk—"

"Funny!" said Bud, for his quick ear had noted the differences between the language of Father and Mother and their associates, and the speech to be heard elsewhere: for example, among the swimmers at the Brandywine . . . "Hain't," the swimming-hole youngsters would say, for

43

"have not," and "ever' " for "every," and "lem me loose" and "pert' nigh"—and a thousand other quaintnesses. So Bud himself would have talked, had it not been for his parents' corrections when his tongue slipped.

And this was *dialect?* He tucked the fact away in his retentive brain. . . .

At noon Father guided the cutter into a small covert off the Pike; he checked Sorrel and put a blanket over his sweating flanks. ("Don't get the wheezes, old horse," he said affectionately.) Then Mother distributed the sandwiches and the slices of pound cake from her hamper. She had brought hot milk, too, in a stone jug swathed in canvas sacking—so hot that when she pulled the cork, a wraith of steam ascended like plumy smoke from the jug's neck.

An hour more of driving and they were in Philadelphia. The village was a mere dotting of dwellings and the blacksmith's shop where Father would transact his business. Mother had a friend in Philadelphia and went there to call. The boys were given liberty to tumble and frolic in the snow.

Johnty had an inspiration. "Let's make a snowman!" But they were just at the start of the project when Father came from the blacksmith's to summon them. It was time, Father said, to turn homeward.

"Shoot!" ejaculated Johnty, disappointed. "We haven't had a decent snowman this year. Wish I'd thought of it sooner."

44

As they bundled back into the buffalo robes, Father said: "The days are getting longer. We shall be in Greenfield before dark. A good thing."

Afterward, Johnty and Bud reminded each other what a *very* good thing it was, for had not spring's lengthening hours of light been at hand, despite the pall of this freakish cold snap, they might have missed a wondrous sight.

They were bowling down Main Street—rapidly, as if Old Sorrel smelled the oats awaiting him in his manger—and clattering to a halt at the fence when they saw it, outlined against the bright red semicircle of the sinking sun.

"Look!" Bud cried. "Johnty! It's the snowman you were wishing for."

"Well, I'll be switched!" exclaimed Johnty.

The figure in the front yard was mammoth, three vast balls of snow piled up to the height of a Goliath. The snowman had features, a jutting nose and jaw, eyebrows and whiskers of thick-curled moss, walnuts for eyes. A wooden gun was set in the curve of his arm, the barrel protruding above his shoulder. About him were crisscrossed tracks of wet black earth that told how he had been made.

"Who did it?" Johnty demanded. "He's a soldier, Bud. A soldier on parade!"

"Someone must have worked for hours," said Mr. Riley.

"Isn't he *sassy?*" piped Bud.

45

"So realistic I'm almost terrified," said Mother, smiling.

They all were standing beside the snowman, awed by his bulk, conjecturing as to who could have planned this surprise. Then Johnty spied someone lurking in the lee of the stable.

"Noey Bixler! Hi, Noey, you did it!"

He had to chase Noah and drag him around to the front yard and fairly ring a confession from him.

"Yes, it was me," Noah admitted, blushing, shifting his big boots, blinking in an agony of self-consciousness. "I come over this morning and found you wasn't here, and the idee struck me."

"But what a job, Noah!" Mother said.

"Yes, ma'am. More'n I contracted fer, in the beginning. Seemed like he jist *grew* on me. I rolled and rolled clean round the house. It was fun. I fergot my dinner and stayed, workin'. I had to hump to git the top-half on the legs-half. It winded me. 'y jingo, I jist drapped down on the stoop and panted like a dog!"

"His hair is so beautiful, his whiskers." Bud was dancing ecstatically around the snowman.

"They're padding out o' buggy cushions. I gouged his face with a trowel for the cheek-bones and nose. I been at it most o' the day."

"Tell Noah how much you appreciate his kindness, boys," said Mother.

"Oh, thank you, Noey!" Their voices were a duet.

"Glad you like him." Noah's plump face creased into

46

a grin. "I jist done it fer old-acquaintance-sake." . . .

All that week and for many days thereafter the snow-man mounted guard between the gate and the house. When the sun had melted other ice and snow and rivulets ran in the gutters, still he stood, a stern, heroic form, alone; thinning, diminishing, yet never losing his grandeur—until at last he faded, and it was really spring.

Chapter Six

SUMMERS WERE ALWAYS eventful and this one of 1855 had joys innumerable. Uncle Mart was in Greenfield most of the time. He made and nailed to the stable a bird-house in which a pair of swallows nested—a remarkable bird-house: not only did it have windows and doors but a veranda and balusters, two chimneys painted crimson and penciled with white lines to look like bricks, and two tiny lightning rods to twinkle in the sun. Also Uncle Mart organized a neighborhood circus. With the help of Johnty and Noah, Almon Keefer and Jim Offutt and other willing workers, he contrived a stage in the stable loft. He never lacked for performers; there were acrobatic Arabs, slack-rope walkers, bareback riders, even an "Injarubber-Man." Bud was the clown and laughed convulsively at his own antics. The price of admission was twenty pins and no patron ever was known to complain that it was excessive.

Trips to the Brandywine were an every-day occurrence. Bud could swim now and was learning to dive. He went to see Irvin Hunt and fished with him. He ranged the creek from end to end with the zeal of an explorer. An even greater pleasure, he thought, was to lie in the sand along the brink where cattails and pennyroyal grew, and there, partly in the water, partly out of it, to listen to Almon Keefer read from *Tales of the Ocean,* or from a book about savage Indians and intrepid scouts. A big boy with a resonant voice, Almon read well, even thrillingly. But after an afternoon of hearing about jolly tars and pirates or the blood-curdling doings of *The League of the Miamis,* Bud often had a night of troubled dreams.

Sometimes he went to Bixler's, to inspect Noah's many pets, the caged squirrels, the stolid owl, terrapins and mud-turtles and the little 'coon whose name was Bolivur. Bud wished that he had a 'coon, and Noah obligingly promised to get him one.

On Saturday evenings Bud liked to go marketing with Mother. He had long ago hoarded the pennies necessary to buy the bar of Pear's soap and was carrying the fragrant red-brown morsel in his pants pocket to perfume his handkerchief. One Saturday while Mother was busy elsewhere, he marched into the general store and bought a pair of boots with brass heels and green leather tops. Jim Offutt

49

had such boots, Bud always had wanted some—he acquired them by saying to the young lady clerk: "Charge 'em to Mr. Reuben Riley." The clerk did not demur. Mr. Riley's credit was still good, it seemed.

Bud didn't wear the boots; they were too pretty for that. He hid them in his room, to gloat over in secret. He loved pretty things! He had now a poetry book, a bar of transparent, sweet-scented soap, the boots. He thought he would like to own a violin, a banjo and a guitar. Then when Mother played the melodeon in the parlor, he could make music too!

He dreaded to see the summer end for in the fall he would have to go to school, or so Father was saying. To Bud this prospect was alarming. . . .

The school was not that which Johnty attended but one for younger children, taught by Mrs. Frances Neill in her little old three-room cottage on the side street. Mrs. Neill was very old herself, and fat and vivacious. Her face was round and smiling beneath a starchy, frilled cap tied with ribbons; she had bright eyes, a large mole on her cheek and a quick, teetering walk, like a robin's. She looked really as if she might be Dame Trot, just stepped from the pages of Mother Goose.

There were twelve boys and girls in her classes; Mrs. Neill referred to them as her "dear tots" or her "scholars." She was tender and forbearing with them, attempting no strict discipline. But she did have certain rules for deportment, and punishments if the rules were broken. A girl who whispered during lessons would have a folded bandage placed on her desk; if the whispering persisted, the bandage would be bound over the girl's mouth and she would have to wear it until recess. A boy who was impudent or rude must have his mouth wiped out with a penholder which had been dipped in ashes. The child who hit or kicked a comrade would be whipped on the foot.

This treatment, the worst in Mrs. Neill's system, always seemed to hurt her more than the scholar upon whom it was inflicted. Tears would glisten in her eyes as she wielded the whip—and then she would invariably lead the offender to her kitchen, a picturesque room, quite like Dame Trot's, and give him a piece of fried chicken or a bun spread with blackberry jam.

Mrs. Neill was not without her peculiarities. For instance, she believed that there were mice in her cottage and she hired a man to come up from town one day each week and walk through the house, beating a drum in every room, to drive the mice away. That no one (and not even Mrs. Neill herself) ever had *seen* a mouse mattered not at all. "Filthy rodents!" said Mrs. Neill. "They are *everywhere.*"

On a baby-blue ribbon around her neck Mrs. Neill wore a silver dollar. This ornament she highly prized; but, being unselfish, she wished others to have the glory of wearing it; and so, on each Monday morning she bestowed it upon that one of her "dear tots" whose deportment had been most exemplary the week before. When

51

the ribbon became too soiled for further use, she substituted a fresh loop, but the color must always be blue, and the temporary possessor of the dollar must guarantee to keep it shining as if new-minted.

Mrs. Neill never owned a school-bell. "I don't *like* the raucous things!" she said. When the children had a breathing spell outdoors or, in bad weather, on the little balustraded back porch, she called them in to their studies by knotting a yellow bandana handkerchief to a pole and waving it at the door vehemently, the while in silence she nodded her bonneted head and smiled broadly.

She often said that she did not believe any girl or boy of the sort who came to her ever was or could be intentionally naughty. "Careless, maybe," she admitted. "But *not* naughty." She loved them all and petted them. If a scholar seemed drowsy, she very sensibly reasoned that he needed a nap *("Poor* child") and dispatched him to have one. Perhaps as a consequence, a percentage of the "tots" got quite drowsy every day; but Mrs. Neill never was known to suspect anyone of feigning.

It might be supposed that in such a school Bud Riley would have been content. Instead, he resented it. He was fond enough of Mrs. Neill herself, for her geniality was not to be resisted; but the lessons she endeavored so valiantly to teach him were a bother. He knew how to read; he finished the *Primer* before his classmates had toiled through the first assignment. The *Primer* seemed unutterably silly to him, and the *First Reader* was worse.

Hoosier Poet

"Is it an ax?
It is an ax.
It is my ax.
Is it by me?
My ax is by me.
So it is."

"Bosh!" said Bud and scornfully flipped the pages. He would rather *never* be decorated with Mrs. Neill's silver dollar than tarry with that stupid numskull and his ax!

The final story in the book was about Willy, Katy, Carry and their mother, who went to the seaside. They dug for shells. (There was a picture of them, digging.) They threw down their wooden spades. Why? Because a ship was sailing by. (There was a picture of the ship and of all the seaside party looking at it.) "Soon the ship will be out of sight," said the *Reader,* "and the children will go home."

Ah, but would they? Bud thought rebelliously that Willy, Katy, Carry and their mother would do nothing of the kind. Go home, indeed! Not unless they were crazy! No, if they had a grain of gumption, they would flag down that ship, stop it, beckon it to them. Then they would embark and, without an instant's hesitation, glide off to foreign strands and pick pineapples and cocoanuts in the tropics.

Having voyaged with the people in Almon Keefer's *Tales of the Ocean,* Bud could not tolerate the insipid Willy and Katy of the *First Reader.*

53

Since he never studied he had much time to waste in pranks. He received whippings on the foot—and pieces of fried chicken. Mrs. Neill mourned over him and implored him to be diligent at his lessons. One day he exasperated her beyond endurance and she said she would have to send him home. Bud was taken aback. This was the last thing he'd reckoned on; he could imagine what Father would have to say about such a disgrace.

Something must be done, and quickly; and so he wailed: "I'm sleepy!"

"Ah?" Mrs. Neill looked relieved. Of course, if the child was sleepy—

She ushered him into the inner room and placed a pallet on the floor. The shades were drawn at the windows, the room was gloomy, and for a moment after Mrs. Neill had bustled out, Bud thought he was alone. Then a movement somewhere disturbed him and he twisted around to see an old man seated in a rocker. His hair was gray; his hands were relaxed on his knees, his feet in carpet slippers.

"Hello," Bud said tentatively. "Who are you?"

"I am Mrs. Neill's husband."

"Oh?" Bud was startled. "Her *husband?*"

"Yes. And you're one of her scholars?"

"I got sleepy," Bud said.

"I understand." The man smiled wistfully. "Mrs. Neill has brought you here to rest? She is so kind, isn't she? Do

54

you know why she has her little school? Because she must support herself—and me. I am blind."

Bud was shocked. He hadn't known, never would have guessed. Dear, brave Mrs. Neill! He was ashamed that he had caused her anxiety.

"I just pretended to be sleepy," he thought. "I was wicked." He would never misbehave again!

It must be said for him that his deportment improved and he was polite and always more considerate of Mrs. Neill as the months passed. But he didn't progress with his lessons; his report cards were disconcerting.

"Why is it?" asked Johnty, who got on well with any study he undertook. "Don't you even look at the books?"

"Not much." Bud sighed. "The only thing I like about school is recess."

He did not tell his brother that he had more than the dislike of school to contend with: the other children at Mrs. Neill's were laughing at him and making fun of his freckles. Some rogue had nicknamed him Spotted Face.

"Look at Spotted Face!" was the chorus echoing in the schoolyard.

Bud hated that!

In the drug store downtown was a bottle with an ultra-marine label on which was stamped in gold: *"Sure cure for moth, tan, freckles."*

He did not have moth or tan; he did not have fifty

cents which was the price written on the label. But he had freckles—and ached to be rid of them. He went into the drug store four times before he found the courage to say to the proprietor: "Charge it." And he wouldn't have dared to anoint himself where anyone else could witness.

He hugged the bottle under his reefer and stopped in an empty barn on his way to school. He doused his hand and rubbed his face—hard, all over. He waited a minute.

If the liquid was all that it claimed to be, the freckles probably would drop off like beads from a raveled string, rattling as they fell. The minute elapsed . . . Well, maybe that was too much to hope for; he might have to use the medicine more than once. But he was positive there must already be some signs of cure.

He thrust the bottle into the hay and ran out of the barn, scudding along the street, slamming into Mrs. Neill's house.

" 'Scuse me for being late—"

"Why, James Whitcomb Riley!" gasped Mrs. Neill.

"What's the matter?" He was perplexed. The children were tittering and grimacing at him.

"Your—your condition? My dear boy, are you ill?"

"No, ma'am."

"Come." Mrs. Neill bobbed out to the back porch, with Bud in tow. She took him to the washbowl, the mirror suspended there.

He raised on tiptoe and saw his face. It was dyed yellow as an Easter egg!

"Now then," said Mrs. Neill. "What is it?"

Miserably he blurted out his confession. "I thought I'd look so nice!"

Mrs. Neill said that perhaps he hadn't read the directions on the bottle. "Perhaps you should have dabbed it on and immediately wiped it off again, with salt water, egg white or something." She got a brush from the cabinet and began to scrub. "I predict that the freckles will come off—and the skin, too!"

It happened. Bud peeled. To his bitter sorrow, there were freckles spangling the brand-new skin. He was doomed to be a Spotted Face.

There was another aftermath when, in the course of a few days, the proprietor of the drug store brought around his bill.

"This has got to stop," Father said. "Do you want to land us all in the poorhouse, Bud?"

"No, sir." Nothing could have been farther from his intent!

"Unless you curb your extravagance that's what you'll do. Suppose everyone in the family purchased anything he had the whim for. In six months I'd have a staggering debt, one I couldn't pay."

"Oh, but you don't have to pay, Father." Bud went on to explain that, how you just said "Charge it," and the storekeeper wrote down some figures in a little book. There was no exchange of money—

"My son," Mr. Riley said, "you have to pay for whatever you get in this life. In coin or work, in remorse or repentance, one way or another, you pay." He paused. "Well, you're too young to understand, maybe. But you've seen the debtors' cell in the county jail, haven't you?"

"Yes, sir."

"Would you like for the sheriff to lock me up in there?"

"No!" Bud shuddered. *"No!"*

"And I shouldn't like it, either. Will you preserve me from that fate?"

"Oh, yes!"

"Then, *no more charging.*"

Gravely Bud pledged himself. "No more!"

Chapter Seven

*T*HERE WAS A sentence in the *Second Reader*
which seemed to James Whitcomb Riley to have
been written about himself:
"Some little boys do not love their books."

Most emphatically this little boy did not; he detested
anything even remotely resembling lessons. His antipathy
for school was to continue long after he left Mrs. Neill's;
in fact, he was never to become fully resigned to formal
education.

For a term or two he was a pupil in the Greenfield
Academy, a private school of which his father was a
director. Then he transferred to the public school, housed
in the old Masonic Hall on the Square. But wherever he
went, his feeling remained the same. He could not fit him-

self into the routine, and soon he quit attempting to and was known to his teachers as that bugbear of the classroom, a clever and mischievous idler.

He was not unpopular with the other boys and girls. He could spin tall and engrossing yarns; he was adept at games and quite fearless and could even straddle a horse and gallop "face backwards"; he knew how to slide a bit of wood under the school clock and so cause it to run faster toward dismissal time. But the authorities despaired of him. Though he read fluently, skimming the hardest texts like a gull in flight, and his penmanship was symmetrically Spencerian, he neglected to learn spelling, geography and history. As for arithmetic:

"You don't know twice ten from twice eternity!" complained one desperate instructor.

This was the plain truth. He didn't know; he didn't care. After sessions at the blackboard, he often had his legs switched, his knuckles rapped or his ears boxed. When he went home and told of such ordeals, even of floggings, his mother wept. But his father said the teacher probably had sufficient provocation.

"Your own fault!" Mr. Riley was on the examiners' committee of the public schools. "This conduct of yours is unpardonable. You're ten years old. High time you buckled down and got some common sense. How, indeed, can you live without an education? How support yourself? You can't pattern your existence after that of—well, of Irvin Hunt, for instance. You're not that sort of person.

You were born into a different station and must equip yourself to shoulder responsibilities. In Greenfield you'll be among intelligent people. There isn't a more up-and-coming community in the country. I've made a place for myself here and you must be able to take it when I've gone."

Then Father would praise Indiana and its public schools which provided education for students from the primary grades to enrollment in the state university at Bloomington.

"And I should like to see you there, in the Law School. James Whitcomb Riley, bachelor of laws!"

At ten, and his ankles smarting from the sting of a birch rod, James Whitcomb Riley groaned. He'd never be a lawyer, not ever. And how stubborn Father was to cling to the thought. But the only possible reply in these circumstances was: "Yes, sir," and the promise to reform.

Just the same, he would run away whenever examinations were scheduled, and this was several times a week. And on Friday afternoons he was nearly always absent from the Masonic Hall, for that was the day for "recitations," when each pupil must rise, advance to the teacher's desk and recite a poem.

Bud's poem was *Casabianca* and he knew it perfectly. "The boy stood on the burning deck—" Bud revered the courage of that dauntless boy! Yet he himself was so terribly shy and he seemed never to conquer the condition. The teacher said he must recite *Casabianca* and he meant to, sometime. But awaking in his bed each Friday morning, he would be seized with stage fright. Could he get up and open his mouth and tell the class, and also visitors, parents or anybody who wanted to attend, of beautiful and bright little Casabianca? "The boy stood on the burning deck—" With gestures, of course, and much emotion. No, Bud Riley could not do it!

What was there then but to play truant at Tharpe's Pond or the Brandywine, where by putting the thought of tomorrow and more tomorrows behind him, he could be very happy?

The real tragedy of school was that he must be indoors, penned in, like the squirrels in Noah Bixler's cage. He was born to be a wanderer, he was sure of that. He was a dreamer. He had none of Johnty's energy or Father's robust temperament. He loved peace, tranquillity, and the chance to pursue all the whimsical fancies that went round and round in his head. He loved nature; his teachers (yes, and Father too) might have been amazed at the range of his knowledge of natural things, of flowers and herbs and trees, of animals and all the insects of meadow and forest. He was acutely aware of details; like blotting paper his memory soaked up and retained impressions of any scene. He could have told the order in which the trees leafed out in the spring, and the birds nested to hatch their young, the varieties of butterflies, the ways of the katydid, the frog, the lightning bug. He knew the look of the sun in each hour of its daily journey, and how the moon waxed from a curved wedge of silver to a milk-white disc in the night sky. He knew the smell of the rain on weeds and on wild roses, of violets and arbutus; and where the best peaches and strawberries were to be found, where water-melons ripened in the patch and luscious pawpaws turned bronze-red in an autumn grove. This was the wisdom which seemed essential to him—and he was gathering it.

Sometimes he reflected that if the school room hadn't had windows he might have been less restless there. But from his seat he could see the National Pike, the steady procession: oxen and mules and donkeys, an imposing coach, a hunter with a deer swinging from the pommel of his saddle, the shambling lines of men with dogs driving hogs and turkeys to market. All the hubbub of the open road drifted in to distract the boy, to set his imagination straying . . .

"Bud Riley? Bud!"

The teacher's voice was irritable and he glanced up.

"I shall call you Jim, henceforth. Bud is too childish a nickname! *Jim* Riley."

"Yes, ma'am?"

"Can you give me the date of Columbus' second voyage?"

No. Nor of the first voyage, either. Who *was* Columbus?

"You don't know even that? How can you be so igno-rant? A boy with your background?"

He flushed, not because the scolding humiliated him,

63

but because he was sorry that the teacher should be cha-
grined. He wanted everybody's good will and believed
that he deserved it. His heart held nothing but cordiality.
He had never harbored an unkind thought or a malicious
impulse. Why, he even liked teachers!

In 1860 he officially discarded the name of Bud and
was known thereafter as Jim. As Father had said, he was
getting on in years. He wasn't the baby of the family now.
There were two children younger than himself in the
Main Street dwelling: a sister, Elva May, who at four
had the blue-eyed daintiness of an elfin creature; and
Alexander Humboldt, the little brother in the cradle. Mr.
Reuben Riley still prospered as an attorney and he must
often have congratulated himself on his foresight in building a spacious home. The Rileys had a "hired girl," Floretty; and a "hired man," Sam, a stalwart country youth
who worked in the yard and the stable.

And there was to be yet another addition to the household . . .

The winter weather was at its bleakest on that day when
the dilapidated farm cart halted at the fence. The man
who climbed over the wheel was gaunt and stooped, with
sallow cheeks and a scrawny beard. At the back door he
asked for Mr. Riley. Standing there in Floretty's clean
kitchen, he was apologetic for the mud on his boots,
obviously ill at ease, somehow abject.

It was evening and Father had just come from the court

64

house. He conferred with the man, and then with Mother. From these conferences Johnty and Jim and little Elva May were excluded. Even Floretty was temporarily shut out of the kitchen, which was her rightful territory.

"What's that fellow want of Father?" Johnty demanded.

"Someone's in the cart," Jim said, his nose flattened against the glass. "It's a woman. No, I think it's a girl. Look! The man's gone out to get her."

"She's coming in!" exclaimed Johnty. "And the man's leaving!"

Mother was at the front door, opening it to the queer, small figure on the threshold. The girl was thin as a reed, and she must have been half frozen, for her dress was of threadbare calico and she had no coat. A shawl was pinned across her narrow chest and she wore an absurd hat, like a straw pancake, bound down over her ears with a shabby green veil. Her lips were pinched and colorless, her hair straggled in a yellow mane over her forehead and about her neck. Yet in spite of her appearance of extreme poverty, the girl carried herself with an air of pride; and when Mother said quietly: "Children, this is Mary Alice Smith; she will stay with us a while," the newcomer smiled and curtsied.

"I'm a orphant," she announced. "I got *no* money an' Uncle Tomps says he cain't afford to keep me no more. So he brung me here to the Rileys."

The arrangement, it seemed, was as simple as that. As

65

Mother later explained to the round-eyed Jim, Mary Alice's Uncle Tomps was penniless and in these straits he had bethought himself of the well-to-do Mr. Riley who had a reputation for being charitable and a friend to the needy. Uncle Tomps had come to beg the Rileys' hospitality for his niece.

"Probably it will be for only a few months, until spring," Mother said. "Let me see. I shall put her in the little rear chamber—"

"Is she really an *orphant?*" queried Jim.

"The word is *orphan,* dear. I don't know. Her mother is dead, but she may have a father somewhere. I'm afraid he has abandoned her."

"Did you see how much she ate at supper?"

Mother nodded. "As if she hadn't had a decent meal in a long time. Poor child! She is fourteen, but not so big as you, Jim."

"I think she's a funny kind of girl," said Jim. "Curious!"

It was a view with which they were all to concur as the weeks passed. Mary Alice Smith was unlike any person they had ever known. She was curious. She had declared at the outset that she would work—"I'll earn my board and keep!"—and she went at her tasks with the fury of a whirlwind. There was nothing she would not do, no service too menial for her to perform; yet she had an imperious, almost queenly manner. And there was the hint of mystery about her; she invested every insignificant act with importance; she whispered and talked constantly to herself.

Before the first day was over she had investigated the house from top to bottom; she knew more about it than any member of the family. The winding stairs in the hall delighted Mary Alice. A dozen times, fifty times, she went up them, stopping on each step, patting the treads softly, resting her face on the carved banister. She said that each step had a name, and when she reached the last one, she paused in the upper hall, and peered down over the railing at Johnty and Jim, awestricken below.

"Where—is—Mary—Alice—Smith?" Her voice had the stretched, shrill sweetness of a flute; she answered her own question: "Oh,—she—has—gone—home!"

Then she descended the stairs. "I'm mighty glad I'm come to live in this-here house. On these-here stairs I can play I'm mountin' up to heaven. But," she said, "some day you'll call me and I won't be here."

"Why?" asked Jim.

"I'll be gone, that's why."

Again and again the strange little drama was enacted, she seemed never to weary of it. "Where—is—Mary—Alice—Smith?" And whether or not anyone watched or listened, the fluting, echoing cry: "Oh,—she—has—gone—*home!*"

She was talkative as a parrot and indulged in long conversations with numbers of fancied characters. For each character she had a different voice and since these unseen companions were for the most part very impolite and quarrelsome, forever chipping in with arguments and contradictions, the conversations were quite spirited. She was content to be alone, sweeping, dusting, making beds or rocking the baby's cradle; yet she liked John and Jim and welcomed their society, especially in the kitchen of evenings, when she usurped Floretty at the sink and transformed the dishwashing into a ceremony.

Then when the plates and cups and saucers had all been wiped until they glistened and put away on the cupboard shelves, she would draw the boys and Elva May and the bewildered Floretty into chairs around the stove, and close the door, and extinguish all but one of the candles.

This was the climax of Mary Alice's day, the hour in which she was her most mysterious, and which Jim had been anticipating.

"I'll sing a ditty," she said, and ran her fingers over an imaginary keyboard. When she had sung, "I'll dance," she said. "I'll be a locomotive. Look! Puff-puff-puff. I'm breathing *fire!* I'm belching *cinders!*"

Next she propounded riddles which only she could solve, though they were "fool-riddles," she said that anybody could guess "with both eyes shut." She told jokes— and stories.

There never had been such stories as those of Mary Alice Smith. Floretty, a wholesome, sensible young woman, protested that they were a "pack o' lies," all about gnomes and ogres, brownies and goblins, and there-

The old swimmin' hole.

fore ridiculous. But this to Jim was their magic. When, seated in the warm, shadowy kitchen where the single candle flickered, he heard Mary Alice speak in her weirdly sweet tones of the fabulous monsters that pounce out "if you don't say your prayers," or "if you mock an' shock the ole folks," Jim shivered and was enthralled. Such monsters were *everywhere,* Mary Alice said, even here in this very house, in the clothes-press and the dining-room cubby-hole.

"And in the rafter-room," Jim supplemented. Hadn't he always known that, anyway?

Mary Alice's exit was as sudden as her coming had been. On a summer morning Uncle Tomps' wretched cart slowed before the fence. His fortunes had mended; he wouldn't bother the Rileys longer with the sheltering of his niece.

Mary Alice shed a few tears as she donned her shawl, her pancake hat, the bedraggled green veil. But as she went down the walk she was smiling—disdainfully, regally, as a queen would smile. At the gate she lifted her hand, fluttered it.

The house was oddly silent that day, and for many days. Prowling through the hall, Jim thought he could catch a shrill, haunting refrain from regions above. "Where—is—Mary—Alice—Smith? . . . Oh,—she—has—gone—home!"

He was never to see her again, and never to forget her.

Chapter Eight

THAT WAS THE year for state and national elections, and Mr. Reuben Riley was a delegate to the convention which nominated Abraham Lincoln as a candidate for the Presidency of the United States. Always before he had been a stanch Democrat in politics, but now that slavery had become an issue, he had embraced the principles of the Republican party. Neither Johnty nor Jim ever would forget the night of their father's return from the convention in Chicago. He had brought little gifts for them and, as they sat up in bed, rubbing sleep from their eyes and hearing the clock downstairs chime twelve, he told them about the nomination.

"It was fine," he said. "Worth going miles to see. The East wanted Seward; but we delegates from the Middle

West and the West wanted *Lincoln,* and no one else would do! Well, we got him. Now we must elect him! Yes, and we must elect Oliver P. Morton as lieutenant-governor of Indiana."

Oliver P. Morton, destined for a great part in his state's history, was Mr. Riley's friend.

The autumn was flurried by political activity. It seemed to Jim that people thought and talked of nothing else. Certainly the Riley house buzzed with it. At barbecues, picnics, at rallies in rural churches and schoolhouses, Mr. Riley was the orator, urging Hancock County to vote for Lincoln and Morton and the Republican ticket.

John, almost sixteen now and a member of the Greenfield Sax-horn Band, often marched in the torchlight parades or was beside his father on the rostrum. Jim would have bartered away everything he owned to have had a similar prominence. As it was, he had to stand on the outskirts of the festivities and watch Father and Johnty nobly upholding the honor of the family. Sometimes he could creep into the procession, just at the very end of it, and snatch up a half-burned torch and brandish the sputtering thing above his head and imagine himself as old enough to be of some importance. Once he was allowed to beat the drum of the Sax-horns. "Boom, boom, *boom!*" The sparks of red fire rained on him, singeing his cottony hair, making little holes in his shirt and roundabout. The fifes squealed in his ears, the brasses blared. "Boom, **boom,** *boom!*"

"Bud," said his mother, afterward, "was it really *you?*"

"It was me."

"The drum was so awfully big. I could hardly see you."

"But you *heard* me, Mother?"

"Oh, yes! Everyone heard. It was enough to wake the dead."

Perhaps, too, Mr. Riley in 1860 was affiliated with the Underground Railroad, that will-o'-the-wisp organization which secretly spirited Negroes out of the South and slavery into the freedom of the North. At any rate, the townsfolk whispered that an agent of the Railroad had been received in Mr. Riley's home.

The agent (if he was that) had been introduced as the Noted Traveler. He must have had another and more specific name, but it was never mentioned. Jim remembered the first time the Noted Traveler arrived, unheralded; a man of sixty, or thereabout, immaculately tailored, his eyes bland and enigmatic behind two pairs of square-framed spectacles, a long-napped white fur hat pulled firmly down over an abundant crop of iron-gray hair. He was reluctant about removing his hat and when persuaded, he kept it near him, balanced on his satchel, which seemed to contain an inexhaustible supply of pamphlets and tracts. Except to Mr. Riley, the Noted Traveler never revealed his mission. The two men would closet themselves behind locked doors, from which mumbled, mystic phrases seeped out—"shibboleth" and "ruthless juggernaut," "emancipate" and "the great battle of Armageddon." Eavesdropping in the hall, Jim wondered as to the meaning of the phrases.

It was Johnty who suggested the idea of the Noted Traveler's identification with the Underground Railroad.

"You know how he talked that night?" Johnty said alertly. "Well!"

Jim recalled the occasion to which his brother referred.

They had been in the parlor, a rather large group: all the Rileys, even to Elva May and Humboldt, the baby. Uncle Mart was there, and Noah Bixler and Almon Keefer, and some adult friends from the neighborhood. Cousin Rufus Hough had drifted in; he was a young law student now clerking in Father's office and adored by both the Riley boys.

The merriment had been spontaneous, just the coming together of congenial people. Mother had played the melodeon and sung; Elva May "spoke a piece"; and little Humboldt ("Hum," they called him) was coaxed to lisp out his story about the bears, which was always such a favorite with the family. Uncle Mart and Cousin Rufus were in fine fettle; everyone laughed at their quips and nonsense. Floretty, entering with a tray of doughnuts and lemonade, had been so entertained that she lingered. Sam, the hired man, sidled in and sat down in an inconspicuous corner.

A pleasant casual evening, Jim would have said, the sort that gave you the feeling of security, of lighthearted mirth—until someone politely asked the Noted Traveler if he wouldn't tell a story, also.

He said instantly that he would. He glanced around the room, fingered his hat as it lay on his satchel. "This is the history of an old Negro woman and her huband and their five sons, how they were slaves and were freed."

At once a serious flavor was injected into the careless fun. As the Noted Traveler went on with his recital of injustices and persecution and race prejudice, Jim had seen his father's countenance darken. With the ending of the anecdote, a strained silence fell. And Jim had been angry with the Noted Traveler for spoiling everything!

Mr. Riley might, indeed, be a foe to slavery; but there were people in Indiana who did not share the sentiment. As he himself had said, the state's inhabitants were a blending; a fair percentage of Hoosiers had a southern ancestry behind them, the traditions of Virginia, Tennessee and Kentucky. They might not own slaves, they might condemn the institution, yet they believed that in the conflict which seemed to be brewing the South had inalienable rights. They foresaw that a struggle might come between North and South, and they feared it.

As the year wore on, and Abraham Lincoln was elected, and also Oliver P. Morton, and all the Republican ticket, and discussion of slavery grew more heated, and a crisis approached in national affairs, Indiana was in a turmoil. Would the South secede? Would there be war? If so, which side would Indiana ally herself with? Surely with the North! And what would southern sympathizers do then?

The winter was increasingly grim and tense in Greenfield, as it was everywhere the length and breadth of the land. Hancock County had sent a company to the Mexican War in 1846, to serve with General Winfield Scott, and knew what war was and why it should be abhorred. But the war which now seemed to impend would be more dreadful, an internal strife, with American contending against American.

Mr. Reuben Riley had implicit confidence in Abraham Lincoln. "He'll steer us through," he said. But other Hoosiers differed. On February 11, Abraham Lincoln made an address from the balcony of the Bates House in Indianapolis. Many of his listeners had misgivings as to his qualifications for the Presidency to which he soon would be elevated; and an Indianapolis newspaper commented editorially that Mr. Lincoln lacked will and purpose, the resolute determination necessary to success; it was doubtful that he would administer the government wisely.

Seven southern states had separated themselves from the Union; on February 18, 1861, Jefferson Davis was inaugurated as President of the Confederate States of America. On March 4, Mr. Lincoln was inaugurated and announced his policy, saying in substance that he would preserve the Union at all costs. On April 14, Fort Sumter was fired upon by the Confederate General Beauregard—and the war had begun.

That very day Indiana made up her mind as to her loyalty. There might be bickerings in some sections, but as a state Indiana was for the President and the Union cause. When, on April 15, the governor called for troops, thousands of men armed for their country's defense.

Mr. Riley's wife and children were not surprised that he promptly volunteered. "What else would you expect?" asked John. "It's just like him," said Jim.

He went headlong into war preparations. Enlistments must be speeded, he said; the county must make a creditable showing. With a fife and drum corps he started on a circuit of Hancock County, with such effect that one week later, on April 22, Company G, 8th Regiment, Indiana Volunteers, was mustered into Lincoln's army. Reuben Riley was the captain; the company had been recruited for a period of three months.

Probably by that time the war would be over.

To Jim the spring was exciting but harrowing. He missed his father. The family circle had been broken; and though the situation might be only temporary, Jim shrank from seeing the empty chair at the dinner table, the shadow in Mother's eyes. It was odd, too, to go down to Father's law office and find Cousin Rufus Hough at Father's desk. The streets were less colorful than they had been, for fewer people were about. At night the Saxhorn Band rehearsed and drilled in the Square to martial music which made Jim's spine tingle, his vision blur. He knew very little of the war, really; he hadn't Johnty's understanding of the underlying reasons for it. But he felt its sadness and foreboding.

When school was out, Cousin Rufus took Mrs. Riley, John and Jim and Elva May on a week-long excursion to Mooresville and Martinsville where they visited the Marines. Driving in Cousin Rufus' carriage, behind his prancing horse, with Elva May on Mother's lap and the boys on little seats that unfolded from the dashboard, they passed the toll-gate with its well-sweep pole and were out in the sun and dust of the National Pike. They went west to Indianapolis, then jogged southward on byroads; Cousin Rufus was cheery and amusing; and at every stop there were Marine relatives, aunts and uncles, to give them bountiful meals and a gala reception.

Then, soon after this interruption of monotony, Mother had the tidings that Company G, the "three months men," had been ordered to the front. They went to bid Father goodbye.

Camp McClellan, where the Greenfield troops had been training, was just five miles outside the city of Indianapolis. It had been hastily built to accommodate inpouring volunteers; conveniences and refinements were few. On that morning when Mrs. Riley led her little brood past the sentries, the camp was in confusion. Tents were being taken down, baggage and ammunition hauled, and the soldiers readying themselves for their march to the railway terminal.

79

The Rileys were not the only civilians in this military scene. Many women and children were there, each family filing in to seek its own hero. The ladies of Greenfield had made a beautiful silk flag for Company G; it was presented to the officers; and a moment of silence and prayer spaced the noise and movement, when everyone, soldiers and guests alike, reflected on the swift-flowing events which had precipitated this emergency, and marveled that a world which had seemed so sane should now be so chaotic.

After the prayer, while Father and Mother and the younger children sauntered to a bench under the trees, Jim and Johnty dodged off through the crowd. As usual, Jim was all eyes and ears, thinking that Father was a gallant figure in his blue coat with the brass buttons, gratified to see how he had been saluted by privates, corporals and sergeants.

"Hey, Johnty, there's Mr. Harris!"

"*Lieutenant* Harris," said John. "Let's talk to him." He touched the sleeve of a man in uniform. "Hello, sir."

Lieutenant Lee O. Harris swung around. "John Riley! And Jim! What do you think of our shindig here?"

"I wish I were going with you," said John.

Lieutenant Harris was one of Greenfield's most distinguished citizens, a poet and a teacher. Jim had known him only casually, nor did he suspect then that in the future their association would be close and intimate.

"I was awakened about three o'clock this morning,"

80

Lieutenant Harris said, "by the blowing of trumpets, the booming of drums, frantic shouts. Such a tumult as I never heard before!—"

"That was because of the orders?" said Johnty.

"Yes. I went to the door of my tent and—you wouldn't have believed it! There was almost the whole company demonstrating patriotism by turning handsprings, somersaults, and whooping at the top of their lungs. And notwithstanding that I'm a sober fellow ordinarily I shouted too!"

"Did Father turn handsprings?" Somehow Jim couldn't imagine that.

"Oh, no. Not Captain Riley." Lieutenant Harris laughed. "With him soldiering is a duty. Your father and all the older men want to have the annoyance of it over and done with, so that they can go home to their normal activities, their businesses. But most of these boys are young; they aren't thinking of enemy cannon, or wounds or sacrifice. War is an adventure to them. I remember how I was at that age."

"You surveyed a route across the continent, didn't you, sir?" said Johnty.

"Yes, with a detachment of United States engineers I went from Pennsylvania to Puget Sound. It was a lark; I never thought of the hazards and hardships."

"Will you be in any fighting?"

"We may, John. We're bound for Camp Benton in Virginia. The fighting isn't far from there."

81

"Mother says you'll all be back by fall, sir." The war did not seem glamorous to Jim; and the prospect of Father or Lieutenant Harris or any of the Greenfield men being in a battle gave him a quaking in his stomach.

"By fall? Yes, we will," Lieutenant Harris said. "Why, I'll have to! My school opens in September. Maybe I'll have you in my class, Jim. John was my pupil, and an enterprising one."

Jim had no time to reply. Just then a bugle blew, the signal for the assembling of the scattered troops—and for the last goodbyes.

The boys scurried to the bench. Father had risen, one arm about his wife, one about Elva May. He kissed them and patted little Humboldt's curly head. He shook Johnty's hand. "I'm depending on you to look after everything while I'm away, John."

"Yes, sir, I will."

"And you, Jim. You must take care of your mother, especially."

"Y—yes, sir," Jim stammered.

"May God bless and keep you," Father said. "My dear ones."

Very erect, he strode toward the ranks.

The "three months men" were to be in the thick of much fighting, to witness suffering and bloodshed, to tramp over battlefields of defeat and of victory. In August, having fulfilled their enlistment contract, they were mustered out of the service.

When news came that Company G was on its way back to Greenfield, the Sax-horn Band rushed out along the road to meet the veterans and pipe them into town with appropriate glory. There was an enormous celebration, for Company G had returned intact, without the loss of a man.

But rejoicing had no place in the Riley household. Captain Reuben Riley was at home—yes, but he had come only to re-enlist, and this time for three years or the duration of the war.

Many of his comrades followed his example. When Captain Riley left again, Almon Keefer and Noah Bixler went with him. And the Sax-horn Band, except for John Riley and one other lad too young, volunteered as a unit and marched away to become the regimental band of the 17th Regular Indiana Infantrymen.

Chapter Nine

THE YEARS OF the war were difficult for Jim. He
was old enough to see its effects upon his country,
his town, those people whom he most loved, yet
too young to have a hand in remedying matters. He
felt helpless, and often hopeless, too. Looking back, he
thought of his childhood as a time of unblemished happiness, but that had been swept away, and he brooded sensi-
tively over the adjustments to be made.

With Father in the army and the income from his law
practice cut off, the Rileys must be very economical. There
was no hired man in the garden now and no Floretty in
the kitchen. Mother did the housework, assisted by John
and Jim. The boys also had to mind the smaller children.
This was a pleasure to Jim, for he preferred playing with

Elva May and little Hum to games with his schoolmates. They were still at an age to believe in fairies and to be spellbound by the stories he told them.

He wasn't faring well with his lessons; he would never be a student. In the classroom he was indolent, preoccupied, looking toward recess, yawning. In fair weather he was outdoors when any chance offered. If rain or storm confined him to the house, he sketched pictures with his crayons or jotted verses in one of his many scrapbooks. He had the desire to own musical instruments and finally got a flageolet upon which he blew and tootled until the neighbors fled inside and slammed their doors and windows.

"That Jim Riley," said one Greenfield resident, "is the plague of the streets. Him and his squeaking horn!"

He could sing innumerable songs and was rather proud of his voice, though with the exception of Elva May and Hum, no one else seemed to appreciate it. He could not read music and had not the inclination or the perseverance necessary for learning the notes, yet melodies fascinated him and, once having heard them, he could repeat them without mistakes. He could fit words to the melodies too, and so compose his own songs, just for the entertainment of himself and his little brother and sister.

He had not forgotten his promise to Father to take special care of Mother. He was with her as much as was possible, and he considered it a triumphant moment when he could make her laugh and dispel the cloud that seemed always to hover behind her gentle gaze. If she was not busy with cooking or sewing, fashioning new garments out of something old and worn, he would beg her to walk in the woods with him. Sometimes they went down to the Brandywine and strolled along the creek banks, and Jim showed her all the points of greatest interest—where the fishing was best, the sycamore log by which the ford was crossed, the swimming-hole, and the rocky inlet where once he had caught tadpoles and a painted turtle.

On such jaunts he felt very close to Mother. They were alike in many ways, two quiet people with the taste for dreaming. Jim could talk to her about what he hoped to be and do. Mother still wrote poems now and then.

"But you have more talent than I ever had, dear," she said. "I think you could be a poet if you tried."

"Really? Like Grandpa Marine?"

"Oh, much better, Jim. Your Grandfather was an amateur. Poetry wasn't a thing he took seriously or worked at. You must have someone else for a model. Some true genius, such as—well, Longfellow."

Jim knew nothing of Longfellow; he seldom read any good books, just newspapers or dime novels. But Mother had read *Evangeline* and *Hiawatha* and *The Courtship of Miles Standish;* to her Longfellow seemed the greatest of American poets. When she had obtained these volumes from the Greenfield library and they had perused them together, Jim agreed that Longfellow must be his ideal. He

86

had no other, for he was too aimless to study without
direction.

The first burst of excitement had spent itself and Greenfield settled down into the dreary rut of war conditions,
living each day as it came, praying for the Union's ultimate victory. The armies of North and South were at
grips. After every battle newspapers were anxiously
scanned. When the name of a Hancock County soldier
was listed among the dead, the wounded or the missing,
there was a general mourning. The families of soldiers
clung to those folk who had similar worries, a bond of
common sympathy.

Mr. Reuben Riley's old mother came to Greenfield
and rented a small house in South Street, just that she
might have the solace of being near kith and kin.

The Riley children loved Grandma. Brisk and agile, she
would walk in upon them almost every evening, bringing
a basket of gingerbread or cake or Bartlett pears. "Treats,"
she said, "for anybody that runs to kiss their Granny!"
But even had she arrived empty-handed, she would have
been kissed and greeted with elation, Humboldt running
into her arms, Elva May exclaiming: "Grandma's come!
Ho, my lawzy-daisy!"

When the treats had been distributed, she would lift
both little ones into her lap and cuddle them. She had a
wealth of stories; some were legends and myths, but more

were historical, based on actual happenings. In story-telling she used big words, never modifying her vocabulary, asserting that the children must enlarge *their* vocabularies.

"Won't hurt 'em to learn," said Grandma.

"She's read *all* books," her littlest grandson was once to comment. "Every kind they is, 'bout the land and sea and nations of the earth. My Gran'ma, she is the historiculest woman ever was!"

Jim most enjoyed Grandma when he went to her house and sat with her, holding her yarn which she was winding from skeins into balls, or watching her at her knitting. Then he would ply her with questions. Shrewd, well-informed, keen, she seemed to have the answer to anything he asked.

Frequently Mother and Granny went to the Masonic Hall to sew for the soldiers. In Greenfield, as in every other community, the women and girls had organized a unit to make such articles as were used by the men in the field, socks, shirts, underwear, bandages, packets of scraped lint. "Comfort bags" were turned out by the dozens; they were envelopes of stout cloth with several pockets for combs, stamps, needles and pins and thread, miniature editions of the Bible. The more daring of the girls had been known to slip letters into the comfort bags, and to get acknowledgments from grateful lads in distant camps.

88

But not all the townspeople were engaged in aiding the Union troops. Like its sister states, Indiana was honeycombed with the furtive workings of the Knights of the Golden Circle, a secret society endeavoring to promote the cause of the South, to release Confederate prisoners in the North, to weaken the morale of civilians in every way, and so to prepare for an invasion of Northern territory by the Southern armies.

As the war lengthened out and was a bloody, bitter struggle, the Knights of the Golden Circle and their supporters were more bold and frank in their efforts. This war, they said, was "unholy and unnatural," and had been brought about by abolitionist fanatics. They proclaimed that the life of a white man was more valuable than that of a Negro, or even tens of thousands of Negroes, and they swore to do everything in their power to stop the furnishing of soldiers and dollars to the Union.

Gradually in Greenfield the Knights emerged into the open. They wore the "butternut" colors as a mark of their sentiments. The women of their families had dresses of a peculiar hue, with decorations and buttons made of the cross-section of a butternut, carved and polished into distinctive ornaments.

At first the "butternuts" were only an annoyance to their neighbors, but when they were resentfully labeled "copperheads," they became more arrogant. Street brawls and fist-fights ensued in the public square; sometimes a brick, a stone or other missile would hurtle out of darkness to destroy the property of a prominent citizen who had denounced the Knights of the Golden Circle.

As a reprisal, the butternut emblems were often snatched from their wearers and "copperheads" soundly thumped. Mass meetings of protest were held. Perhaps it was due to the growing violence of the Knights that Captain Riley was furloughed home to speak at several of these meetings. Anyway, more than once, he fleetingly returned and, from goods boxes on street corners or at bunting-draped sessions in the Greenfield Armory, implored his friends to sustain their trust in the Union.

All this agitation was perplexing to Jim and contributed to his feeling of insecurity. How fantastic that people he had known always and liked should now be enemies, opposed to those things which he, as Captain Riley's son, believed in. What was the sense in that? If the "butternuts" were doing what they thought was right, he, for one, could not hate them. Every person must act now as his conscience dictated; but all consciences were not the same.

His brother John was more stern in judgment. John despised the "butternuts," and everything pertaining to them or suggestive of them. There was a time when the two boys must put their differing views to a test. . . .

On a Saturday afternoon they went to see why Grandma Riley had for three evenings failed in her customary call. Could she be ill, they wondered. They had been told that

90

Uncle Mart was in town, which might account for Granny's absence.

Her door was bolted, but they knocked and soon Granny was peeping out at them.

"Oh, it's you?" She grudgingly admitted them. "Martin's here. I've been feeding him and I daresay there's a snack for you."

Uncle Mart was in the kitchen, and he seemed rather nervous, hitching at his suspenders, glancing apprehensively at Granny. "Hi, kids," he said, and gave them cider and crullers and a bite of cold fried chicken.

Jim, glancing up, saw a look pass between Uncle Mart and Granny—a look of something like warning.

"Gobble your rations," Uncle Mart said, "and I'll walk home with you. Better hurry!"

They sat on stools and they gobbled—Jim with such strict obedience that he choked and had to be whacked on the back. But why should there be the need for haste?

Then in the next room someone coughed.

"Who's that?" Jim said.

To his consternation, Granny flung her apron over her head and began to sob. "Oh, dear! Oh, dear!"

Uncle Mart stood up. "Don't fret, Mother," he said. He turned to his nephews. "You may as well know. Your Uncle John Riley is in there." He paused. "This John Riley is my brother, your father's brother—"

"And my son," murmured Grandma from beneath her apron.

"He's a surgeon," Uncle Mart said, "in the Confederate army. He was captured by a squad of federal artillerymen and imprisoned at Alton, Illinois. He has escaped and is a fugitive. Somehow he came to Greenfield. Mother is hiding him until nightfall when he can get away."

John and Jim were standing now, staring round-eyed.

"A Confederate!" John said.

"He's lived in the South ever since he was a very young man and he has chosen to serve it in this war."

"But, Uncle Mart," John said, "that's—that's treason, isn't it, for Granny to keep an escaped Southern prisoner hidden in her house?"

"Many people might think so." Uncle Mart frowned. "Yet she surely couldn't do less. He is her own son. What's your notion? That she should surrender him to the constable? Do you want to have your kinsman incarcerated in a dungeon simply because he has been a patriot?"

"Patriot!" John cried. "He isn't!"

"Oh, yes, he is. According to his lights, he's as much a patriot as your father. And his mother has just as much affection for him as for her other sons." Uncle Mart was very earnest, displaying a trace of the Riley eloquence. "Do you really blame your grandmother for sheltering him, protecting him from his pursuers?"

John gaped, and said nothing. But Jim abruptly burst out:

"No! No, I don't blame her, and neither does Johnty. Granny couldn't do anything else. Not anything!"

"Good for you, Jim! And you'll keep mum about it, will you."

"Yes. I won't tell a soul. And Johnty won't."

"Oh, thank you!" Grandma wiped her tears on her apron. "Thank you, my dears! And now you must see him." She bustled out of the room.

The man who came in with her was disconcertingly like Captain Reuben Riley in face and figure; but his uniform was a tattered gray and he looked thin and harassed. He seemed not at all afraid that the boys would betray him. "I've always wanted to know you," he said. "I wish you could know my children. It is too bad when families are so separated that their members seldom meet. I should be happy to pay my respects to your mother—if things were not so muddled." His eyes softened. "And if I could clasp your father's hand once more!—"

A little later, as they were going home, John said: "I never supposed Granny was a butternut."

"She isn't!" Jim said instantly. "She's for the President, the Union, the North."

"She's doing something that only butternuts do."

Jim had one of his rare flashes of anger. "Would Mother call in the constable to get you or me, if either of us disagreed with her or with each other? Granny is good, Johnty."

"Yes, I know she is. I didn't really mean she was a butternut."

"Maybe some of the rest of the butternuts are good,"

93

Jim ventured. "Wrong in what they're doing—but good at heart."

"No!" said Johnty. *"No!"*

"But you *won't* tell about this afternoon?"

"Didn't I say I wouldn't? Have I ever gone back on my word?"

Jim's anger subsided. Johnty was absolutely reliable, his word had the weight of gold.

During the night and the next day Jim thought a great deal about the fugitive, and hoped that no one else had known of his presence in Grandma's house, and that he had got safely away. When Grandma's evening calls were resumed, he was reassured and soon the incident was only a memory.

There were other incidents. On a hot July morning in 1863, Greenfield was plunged into suspense by the rumor that General John Morgan, the raider, had crossed the Ohio River and was on his wicked, rampaging way through the state, spreading havoc in his wake. No Southern leader was so much feared as Morgan; his method of warfare was to steal and pillage and lay waste the countryside and, like a cyclone, leave disaster behind him.

Hancock County had a homeguard comprising the older men, the young boys and those veterans who had been invalided and discharged from the army. This "Hancock Battalion" had been drilling in a meadow at the edge of town, with Mr. Lee O. Harris as its captain. When he received the message of Morgan's swing into Indiana, Captain Harris marshaled the Battalion and moved toward the scene of the skirmishing. For a week he trailed the Raider, until John Morgan was out of range and over the border, into Ohio. The Greenfield men performed well under stress, but eight were killed and twenty wounded.

In the autumn Captain Reuben Riley was at home once again, urging enlistment, advocating the raising of a bounty for any volunteers who would respond to President Lincoln's most recent appeal for soldiers. Father was leaner now, his hair streaked with gray; and this time he was recovering from a wound. Often, after Father's departure, Jim would lie in bed at night in his garret chamber under the eaves and wonder whether, with the war so awfully long, Father's luck could continue. The slender, somewhat delicate fourteen-year-old boy had the feeling that ill fortune might be just beyond, ominously stalking. Premonition, perhaps—or merely a superstitious flight of his incorrigible imagination. If only the fighting would end!

It did, of course, finally. Greenfield celebrated the news of the fall of Richmond with a huge bonfire on the common; and when, at Appomattox Court House, Robert E. Lee surrendered to Ulysses S. Grant, all Hancock County indulged in an orgy, with barrels of cider and kegs of whiskey brought up from cellars and opened on the sidewalks, there to be upset by the careenings of wagons and drays which bumped over the curbs and by the surging mob of screaming, whistling pedestrians. Hats were thrown into the air; shotguns loaded with paper wads were exploded indiscriminately, and half the revellers were so peppered with the paper shot that for a week afterward they were busy "picking war bulletins" out of their arms and legs and ankles. But not that or anything could have deterred the mad extravagances of people to whom this was the most joyful day of their lives.

The war was over—and Father had come back to stay. He had survived, he had no further wounds, and yet the dreadful four years had exacted a penalty from him. For now he was a man without means, without a business. His law practice had languished, all his clients slipping away to other attorneys; his savings had been long ago exhausted in providing for his family; he had literally no money. He said he would commence the tedious process of building up his practice again. He went every morning to his office, waiting for employment. But none materialized.

He was poor, he was penniless. And there were complications: in the past he had lent his name as a guarantee for the debts of several of his friends; he had signed notes and bonds. When the friends failed in their obligations, the creditors looked to Mr. Riley for payment. He was an honorable man, always had been—

96

"I shall have to sell the house," he said. "What else can I do? We can live with my mother. She will take us in."

But Grandma's house was so little! Jim didn't see how they could all squeeze into it. Father and Mother, Johnty, Jim, Elva May, Humboldt—and there was a new baby, too; a sister, Mary Elizabeth. These seven, and Granny herself.

"Don't grumble," admonished Father. He was often curt and brusque in his speech now. "You can thank your stars to have a roof of any kind over your head."

They had to sell most of the furniture also, and every-thing else of value which could be converted into cash. The sunny time of the Rileys' prosperity had been eclipsed by black poverty.

On the day when Jim trudged out of the yard and saw the possessions of the new owners stacked on the grass, to be installed in the rooms which had been so precious to him, he felt that he had plumbed the depths of sorrow. He was carrying his few books, his box of crayons, a fish-ing pole, his Sunday suit in a bundle, and a Maltese cat which was his pet.

He walked across the street, stopped, and looked back. He had loved that house. Every detail of it, inside and out, he would remember always, and all the people to whom it had been home, and the fun they had known there, together.

"Sometime *I'll* buy it," he said slowly, under his breath. "Sometime it will be mine again."

97

*F*ITTING THE SEVEN Rileys, with their belongings and the cat, into Grandma's cottage was just
as Jim had thought it would be: not easy for any
of them—and probably not easy for Grandma, though she
never grumbled. To help with the family's finances, John
took a job; but Father said that Jim must keep on with his
schooling.

"As I see it, you have a minimum of book-learning,
Jim; and you show no aptitude for any sort of work. Or
maybe you'd like to read law with me."

"No, thank you." Jim sighed. "I'll go to school."

He was sixteen, not tall or muscular, but weedy, rather
pale, still freckled and blond, still an idler at lessons. The
fact that he was older than his classmates was an embar-

rassment which he disguised by being gruff and noisy and prankish. He would sit at his desk, his textbook propped before him, and on his knees, fastened by a neat contrivance of rubber bands, another book—this one a paperbacked novel—which he read intently. If the teacher seemed suspicious and came to investigate, Jim had only to release the tension of the rubber and the novel would snap into his desk and out of sight. He had many such tricks by which to avoid study.

After school he would lounge about downtown, wasting time. One day he drifted into the shop of Tom Snow; the place became a kind of headquarters for him.

Tom Snow was a cultured Englishman who had emigrated to America and invested a considerable inheritance in a tract of land near Greenfield. The purchase was most unwise, the land only a spongy swamp on which no crops would grow. After a season or two of disappointments as a farmer, the Englishman opened a shoe-shop in the town. A philosopher and a Christian, he hung a framed motto over his door:

WOULDST HAVE A FRIEND? WOULDST KNOW WHAT FRIEND IS BEST?
HAVE GOD THY FRIEND: HE PASSETH ALL THE REST.

This was the cobbler's simple creed.

He was by instinct and habit a reader of worthwhile literature, and it was not long before he had added some shelves of books to his walls; presently he had got to be the custodian of the township library. These volumes he kept with his own and the entire stock was freely available to borrowers.

In London, Tom Snow had been a member of clubs where clever young men congregated to discuss authors and literary projects, or to play checkers and chess. That, he thought, was a profitable type of recreation and one which he would be glad to sponsor. He was aware of his limitations; but he did what he could. In a corner of his shop was a checkerboard table; he collected magazines and newspapers; and he encouraged the youths of Greenfield to drop in at any hour. Big and burly-shouldered, with a shock of grizzled hair and a winning smile, he sat, humped over his bench, his leather and lasts and awls, and conversed knowingly of art or fiction or the drama. His "club" might be cramped and littered, the plaster stripping from the ceiling, the floor strewn with trash; but Tom, once launched upon a favorite topic, could ignore all this—and so, too, could the Greenfield boys who came to see him. He was their guide, their mentor and oracle.

When Jim Riley first began his visits to the cobbler, Tom Snow was reading and discoursing upon the novels of Charles Dickens. There, he declared, was a real writer, a genius!

"You're familiar with Dickens' books, Jim?"

"No," Jim said, "I'm not."

"What!" Tom was scandalized. "Why, my lad, he's the greatest novelist in the world! The showman of literature!

He draws the curtain and there is London, its streets and alleys, its aristocrats and beggars and thieves, every phase of its many-sided life. You cannot afford to neglect Dickens . . . But what, pray, *have* you read?"

As Jim enumerated the books he had liked, Tom looked pained and shook his head. "You're on the wrong track. No, no, this will never do! You have a good mind, but you are selecting bad food for it. You'll starve your intellect. Mend your ways before it's too late!"

Though he laughed at such earnestness, Jim took Tom's dog-eared copy of *Old Curiosity Shop* home with him, and then *Martin Chuzzlewit* and *A Christmas Carol.* He understood at once the reason for the cobbler's enthusiasm. These were stories rich in humor and pathos, vivid with description and exciting, well-knit plot. Their author was, as Tom had said, a master, a true genius.

Tom told Jim much about Dickens, how wretched the writer's childhood had been, how he had struggled with adversity and drudged at gruelling tasks he loathed.

"*David Copperfield* is Charles Dickens himself, to an extent. The first chapters of the story will rend your heart with pity for him. But don't be too sorry for either David or Charles. Rather, you must admire them, because both had the vision of what they wanted to accomplish; and they ploughed through every difficulty to success. Dickens had grit—and he sore needed it! Yet now he's at the top of the ladder. I wish," Tom said, "I could have heard him lecture when he was in this country. He goes about, you

101

know, reading from his novels, interpreting them, portraying the characters. He's as much the actor as the writer, in fact. His audiences are always wild with delight. When he appears in a hall or opera house, they have to hang out the 'Standing Room Only' sign, my lad! Ah, he's the marvelous one!"

Jim Riley read *David Copperfield,* and its impact upon him was more profound and far-reaching than Tom Snow could possibly have estimated. Nor did Tom realize that what he had said of Dickens' lecture tours would so much impress his listener. Often in the years to come, Jim would ponder the idea, for it seemed to him that, like Dickens, he also had the twin talents of writing and acting. And though as yet no one believed in him (no one at all, except perhaps his mother) he had felt the stirrings of ambition. How splendid it would be to stand before a cheering multitude and interpret the characters which he alone had created! Maybe some day—

Now Dickens was enshrined with the poet Longfellow in Jim's reverence; and good reading became a requirement. He had seen the difference between such books as *The League of the Miamis,* a cheap tale of hair-breadth western adventure, and novels of high quality; he would never more be satisfied with the second-rate. He found an old satchel in Granny's woodshed and seldom left home without it, for he must have a convenient receptacle for the half-dozen volumes to be lugged back and forth from the township library. He read Washington Irving's

102

The Sketch Book and *The Alhambra,* the novels of James Fenimore Cooper, *Don Quixote, Robin Hood, Robinson Crusoe, The Swiss Family Robinson,* Weem's *Life of Washington.* Indeed, he went straight through the three hundred books which made up the library, and some he read again and again. *The Arabian Nights* he knew almost by memory, page for page.

Then Tom Snow lent him a set of books, *The Lives of Eminent British Painters and Sculptors.* In these accounts of the obstacles which Sir Joshua Reynolds and Gainsborough and Romney and West, and all the other great artists, had met and overcome as they progressed from obscurity to fame, Jim discovered an inspiration which was to endure. As he finished each story, Jim compared himself with its subject. What one man had done, another could do. Surely!

"I'm going to be famous," he said, softly to himself. "Yes, I am. Famous."

And yet he wavered. Idleness had a very firm hold upon him. He could cast it off, but it would return. He could erect air-castles, but he had not the strength of will to make his dreams come true. He was gentle and shy, amiable and eager to please. He detested all forms of physical exertion or manual labor. At any time he could be led by gay companions from work or study to sports and diversion.

His ambition was as unsteady as his will power, and

103

the fame he dreamed of had varying aspects. Sometimes he saw himself as an artist or cartoonist, sometimes as a musician. Or he might go on the stage. Or be a novelist. Or a poet—like Grandpa Marine, like Mother and Uncle Mart—and Longfellow. Eventually he always came back to poetry.

Probably if he could have talked with somebody, he could have decided as to his future. But he never had confided in any person other than his mother, and now she was ill. Constantly worrying about her frail health, Jim would not bother her with vexing questions. He shrank from consulting with Father, for Mr. Riley's notions as to what Jim would do and be were quite fixed.

At eighteen he was still in school, still dawdling. But now he had a new teacher, one he respected, Lee O. Harris.

Captain Harris (in civil life he had retained his military title) was a man of perception who saw beneath Jim's rough surface to his tender, sensitive heart. He sensed the gropings of this wayward, shabbily-clothed boy toward some kind of self-expression, his desire to be out of the humdrum existence he was leading. Captain Harris thought it was an error on the part of the boy's father to force him to go to school when he had such an aversion for it. Though he couldn't interfere directly, Captain Harris tried to make Jim's path a little smoother. He invited Jim to come to his home and to "loaf" with him on

104

Saturdays. Captain Harris drew him out about his love for Longfellow's poetry; he introduced Jim to the songs and ballads of Robert Burns. Captain Harris was himself a poet of more than local prominence. He read his own verses to Jim and flattered him by asking for his opinion and criticism.

Soon the relationship between the two was that of friends rather than of instructor and pupil. Captain Harris did not attempt to discipline Jim. He suggested that if Jim must play the trick with the rubber bands he had better substitute some standard work for the disappearing novel.

"Oh, I've done that, sir," Jim said, with his guileless grin. "I've got a biography of Daniel Boone here."

"Excellent!" said Captain Harris. "You must give the class a brief review of it."

Captain Harris was much interested in amateur theatricals and often wrote comedy skits or patriotic dramas which he then produced in the auditorium of the Masonic Hall. He induced Jim to join his troupe of amateurs, and Jim was always fine in his performances. Of course, he had stage fright in the wings; but once before the footlights, he forgot that in the rounds of applause accorded him. In Captain Harris' play *Child of Waterloo,* Jim had the role of "Troubled Tom." This name seemed so appropriate to him that he adopted it for a while and used it as a signature to his letters.

105

Captain Harris tried another plan to rouse this Troubled Tom from his apathy. He chose him as editor of *The Criterion,* the high school paper.

"Look here, Jim," he said. "I can't get algebra into your head, or even plain arithmetic. They won't be tamped in. History is to you a dry thing without juices, dates melt out of your brain as quickly as tin foil on a red hot stove. But you *must* accomplish something constructive. Run *The Criterion* for me."

Jim ran it, for two issues. At the top of the editorial page he inscribed *Veni, vidi, vici;* the dozen sheets of foolscap were pencilled and bound into a pamphlet. Every item in it he had written himself, including three stanzas of verse on the last page which he read aloud to the student body.

That was in the spring of 1870, just before the final examinations. Jim was nineteen and should have been graduating. But the grades of his examinations spelled his doom. . . .

One morning he went into the garden where his father was hoeing the vegetable beds.

"I've quit school, Father." He said it baldly, without any preface, biting his lower lip to conceal its trembling.

Mr. Riley glanced up. "Until next term, you mean."

"No, I've quit forever. I can't go on. There's no earthly use."

"And what will you do? Work?" Mr. Riley's tone was

sarcastic and he handed Jim the hoe. "Let's see you lick into this job." He watched a moment. "Don't like it much, do you?"

"I hate it," Jim muttered sullenly.

"And you're not a good gardener. You're a shiftless, lazy fellow, Jim Riley. No good at anything. I'm ashamed of you—"

Abruptly Jim interrupted the tirade. He threw the hoe into the middle of the garden; he leaped the fence and stamped off down the street. But in less than an hour he was back, leaning over the fence, gazing at his father who had picked up the hoe and was digging with it.

"I'm sorry, Father."

Mr. Riley was white with rage. "Sorry?"

"Because I was so rude. Forgive me. But I—I can't—" He stopped, his voice breaking.

There was a silence, and then Mr. Riley said: "My son, whether you believe it or not, I want you to be happy."

"Do you? I'm not. I'm miserable!"

"I can see that. And I don't know what to make of the situation or of you." Mr. Riley rubbed his forehead. "Well, Jim, maybe you ought to go your way, and I'll go mine."

"Yes, sir," Jim said.

But what was his way? Baffled, he asked Tom Snow, and the cobbler said that Jim could be a clerk in the shoe-shop. But then Tom Snow died, and his shop passed into other hands, to someone less well-disposed toward Jim. And a greater tragedy impended.

Jim's mother died.

His grief was immeasurable. He had loved her so dearly. They had understood each other, had been bound by a mutual tenderness. He would never again care for anyone as he had cared for her.

He was stupefied, and then desperately anxious to leave Greenfield, to put miles between himself and all the things which would remind him of his loss. Where could he go? In Rushville, a man was advertising for an agent to sell Bibles. Jim went there, took the agency, and for weeks canvassed the town, the county, from house to house—and sold not a single Bible. He was forlorn, unkempt from sleeping in barns, haymows, anywhere he could lay his head. He was hungry. That, in the end, drove him back to Greenfield. He was so hungry!

"Father," he said humbly, "I must do something."

"I wish to heavens you would, Jim!" Mr. Riley was grim, yet pitying.

"Anything!"

"If you feel like that, you can get a job. I know where there's a house to be painted. I'll buy you the paint and the brushes. Whatever you earn is yours."

Afterward Jim said that the walls of the house seemed vast as a continent. For days he sloshed paint, one coat, two coats, trimmings on shutters and cornices and doors.

The weather was cold, his hands were stiff, the wind whistled through his thin jacket.

On an early January afternoon, as he balanced on the ladder, his brush poised, he saw John Keefer, Almon's brother, on the pavement below.

"Hi, John!"

"What's this?" His friend chuckled. "Work finally caught up with you, did it?"

"Yep, I'm not the gentleman of leisure any more."

"Why don't you try my line? There's money in it," Keefer said.

"Sign painting? I don't know how."

"Shucks! It's mostly just neat lettering. I thought you always bragged about being an artist, Jim."

"Well," Jim said, "I am, and that's no lie. Six years ago, when I was a little shaver of fourteen, I painted a portrait of my father sitting at our fireside. It was pretty good, too."

"Then you could be a crackerjack at signs. Come and let me teach you," Keefer said.

"I may." Jim nodded musingly. "By jingo, I just may!"

Chapter Eleven

*H*E WAS AN apprentice sign painter.

John Keefer's "studio" was situated near the railroad tracks, a cavernous and echoing room in a disused granary. A jolly family of Negroes occupied the adjacent apartment, and when Jim had spare moments from his practice in graining, penciling and landscape sketching, he would talk with the little pickaninnies, amused by them, and often joining in their boisterous games.

Mostly, though, his time was taken up with the work which Keefer assigned him. From the very first, his employer was pleased with Jim's ability. He painted a picture of a greyhound that, Keefer declared, was so perfect that "children going by will be afraid of the dog." He kept regular hours at the "studio" and never shirked.

110

In fact, he had turned over a new leaf, and the gossiping small town of Greenfield soon realized this. His friends were quick to praise him and show their approval of his changed ways. His father was astonished and gratified. Captain Harris beamed upon him. All these evidences of cordiality were balm to Troubled Tom. But even more rewarding was the feeling of self-respect which came to him. Now he had independence—and a few dollars to clink in his pocket on pay day. He did not save his earnings, as his father continually advised; he spent them with a flourish. Economy, if he was ever to learn it, must be a later lesson. It was enough now to be supporting himself, and in a congenial trade he liked.

When several months had elapsed, John Keefer acknowledged that he had nothing more to teach his apprentice. "I could take you on as a partner, Jim; you're that good. But honestly I think you should be in your own business. Why not start in for yourself? I'll stake you to the cost of a kit and paint pots."

The offer was too generous to be refused. Jim began his own business. To publicize the event he painted a distinctive and elaborate sign with his name blazed across it, each letter depicted as the figure of a person—a man, a woman or a child. The sign which proclaimed "J. W. Riley" to be a "House, Sign & Ornament Painter" was so ingenious that the Greenfield postmaster allowed Jim to hang it in the postoffice where it attracted much attention and won him many patrons. In the spring of 1871 he

111

worked at an almost feverish pace; fences and barns in increasing numbers blossomed out with specimens of his whimsical, homely art. A device peculiar to Jim was to rhyme the advertising matter which he placed below the pictures in his signs. He could always find occasion for rhyming—in his work as in his daily life.

Though no one except himself, and perhaps Captain Harris, surmised it as yet, Jim Riley was committed to poetry. To write it would now be his chief ambition. He couldn't have told when the ambition, once so vague and formless, had crystallized into an impelling urge—whether long ago, as he rambled with Uncle Mart or with Mother on the green brink of the Brandywine; or at some later time, under Captain Harris' tutoring, or as he digested Tom Snow's sage counsel. Perhaps he had never forgotten Grandpa Marine. At any rate, the twenty-one-year-old Jim was determined to enroll himself among the American poets. Secretly he was already making steps toward that achievement.

In September, 1870, some stanzas entitled *The Same Old Story,* by "Edyrn" had been printed in the *Greenfield Commercial;* these were followed by *Philiper Flash* and *A Backward Look.* The poems caused speculation. "Edyrn," as many readers of the *Commercial* knew, was the name of a knight in Tennyson's *Idyls of the King,* but no one could guess who this modern versifier might be.

At another time Jim probably would have identified himself as "Edyrn"; but just then he had been submerged

112

in his grief for his mother, and in the multiple woes of the strife with his father, and in the failure of the Bible selling in Rushville. Of course, he read the poems—over and over again!—and pinched himself, scarcely believing they were his own. But he was silent.

In print, his rhymes looked queer, and he could see that they were flawed; yet he was not ashamed of them. Far from it! They seemed to him to be the kind of poems which the average newspaper reader would like. Even then he was thinking that poetry should not be written in lofty phrases. His things, like the songs of Robert Burns, would be not only for the intellectuals, but for anyone who read at all.

As "Edyrn" bobbed in and out of the *Commercial* columns, Jim's ambition soared beyond Greenfield. His brother John was living in Indianapolis. Jim wrote a letter to him: would Johnty censor the spelling of the manuscripts enclosed, copy them in his best copper-plate hand, and then submit them to an Indianapolis editor? The verses must be signed Jay Whit. Jim thought the editor wouldn't reject them. But if he should—"Let me down gently!"

Obligingly, John complied with the request and took the verses into editorial sanctums. He persevered; perhaps as a result, *Man's Devotion,* by Jay Whit, was printed in the *Indianapolis Mirror* on March 31, 1872.

Jim was exultant. "Dear Bro., *you're a good fellow!*"
In May the *Mirror* printed Jay Whit's *A Ballad.*

113

But the author's fervor was a bit dimmed in this case, because both John and the printer had made corrections in the lines. As Jim pointed out, *A Ballad* had been a very special composition, a fragment patterned after the medieval, and Burns; John was wrong to have censored it so much. Also Jim had wanted the poem to have a place on the front page of the paper. He had told John it must be there—or nowhere else. All in all, the publication had not fulfilled his hopes.

However he thanked John, and softened the rebuke by saying with an air of stateliness that "you can't make a silk purse out of a pig's ear," and that he wasn't so vainglorious as to expect to "beat a pathway on to wealth and fame" in a minute or two.

He went on writing. Now in the little satchel from Granny's woodshed he carried pads and pencils; and Greenfield people were to remark upon his way of picking up stray slips of paper in stores or offices, anywhere, and the vacant stare in his blue eyes as he paused in the street to scribble some rhyme or couplet.

"Jim Riley? Yes, I know him," one old lady said. "I've known him and his folks always and well. Whit, they call the boy sometimes; and it used to be Bud when he was a tow-headed tyke. Seems he's getting started at sign painting, but he's a flighty one. You never could put your finger on him, so to speak. Wouldn't surprise me if he up and flew the track. Tomorrow, or maybe *today.*"

His whiskers seemed to wave in the wind.

Hoosier Poet

On a bright summer morning in 1872, Greenfield was enlivened by the arrival in the public square of Doctor S. B. McCrillus of Anderson, Indiana, who drove his big, glitteringly decorated wagon straight up to the courthouse, where he dismounted, hitched his team to the rack and greeted his many acquaintances.

Doc McCrillus was a "medicine man." For years he had peddled his "Popular Standard Remedies" in Hancock County; his name was a household word in Greenfield. Huge and vigorous, ruddy-complexioned and strident-voiced, he fairly exuded health and good humor. His costume was always "a sight for sore eyes," Greenfield people said. Now he was wearing a flashy embroidered waist-coat, open-necked shirt with a flowing silk tie, and fawn-colored trousers strapped into shiny boots. On his head was a Mexican sombrero beneath which his white hair belled out in curls, almost hiding the pearl in a gold loop which was screwed into the lobe of his left ear. His whiskers were white and curly, too, so luxuriant that they seemed to wave in the wind.

Among the friends whom Doc McCrillus spied that morning was a Mr. Derby who had frequently purchased the Remedies. Indeed, Mr. Derby had been a sufferer from stubborn rheumatism until Doc had rescued him—"I yanked you back, didn't I, Derby, from the abyss of pain?" Doc was wont to say. Now the two, sufferer and rescuer, shook hands, and Mr. Derby turned to indicate a companion.

"This is Jim Riley, Doc. You'll remember Captain Reuben Riley?"

"Do I remember Reuben Riley?" Doc's whiskers quivered with emotion as he clapped Jim on the shoulder. "My boy, your pa is the most eloquent orator in the state. Yes, sir, I tell everybody so, and I repeat it. *The* most eloquent orator in Indiana. When he speaks you know that God moves in a mysterious way. You can see Him in the tempest, in the flames of devouring fire. You can hear Him in the earthquake." Doc paused. "Do you make speeches, too?"

"No," Jim said. "I paint signs."

"A splendid vocation! I have a great regard for a talented sign painter. *Are* you talented?"

"Very," said Jim. "Maybe in your travels you need a sign painter, Doctor?"

"I could not get along without one. And," Doc said, with a large gesture toward the wagon, "I have one. Mr. James McClanahan is with me at present, under contract to tour for the entire summer."

Looking up, Jim saw a husky young man in overalls on the wagon seat. The young man winked.

"With a business as enormous as yours I should think you'd need a second sign painter," Jim said.

Doc McCrillus considered this. "Well, my dear Mr. Riley, perhaps I do. I am anticipating a *very* successful season. Yes, I *might*—" He eyed the horizon thoughtfully. "But I have seen no samples of your work."

118

"By what road did you drive in? Past the bridge? Then you must have noticed some displays on the barns. A dove with an olive branch? An eagle and the flag?"

"Yes, I did. Yes, and they were *wonderful.*"

"They were mine," said Jim.

"Yours?" Doc McCrillus glanced at him, more inquisitively. "So you want to travel with me?"

"I do, sir."

"My excellent young Mr. Riley," roared Doc McCrillus, "you are *hired.*"

Within the hour the ornate wagon was stopping at Mr. Reuben Riley's door and Doc McCrillus was saying: "The idea originated with your son, but I endorse it. He has *your* genius, sir, only manifested in a different sphere of endeavor. With your permission—"

Mr. Reuben Riley's smile was a mite constrained. "I was afraid he'd break over the traces. Yes, Doctor McCrillus, if you can make anything out of him, take him along."

The medicine man's span of sorrels bore Jim briskly away to far places and adventure. As a little boy he had loved to sit and watch the pageant of the National Pike. Now he had been set free to journey down the Pike and other roads, traveling in comfort and even in style, for Doc McCrillus' wagon, christened the Buckeye, was new and commodious and equipped for any variety of weather, with curtains to shut out the rain and buffalo robes for the chill breezes that might blow. The seats were cushioned and there was plenty of space behind and around them for the stock of bottles and tins and boxes which contained the Popular Standard Remedies. Doc McCrillus estimated his stock as being worth a thousand dollars and boasted grandiloquently that, so fortified, he could cure any or all of the ills which man falls heir to.

They went straight from Greenfield to Anderson, stayed there a week while Doc made a few final arrangements, and then struck out on a trip which took them clear around the state. For Jim this was an interval of unclouded pleasure. He had instantly been drawn to James McClanahan, the other sign painter of the entourage. Mac was a witty fellow who did not know that such a thing as care existed in the world; a laughing, merry vagabond by nature, a singer of ribald songs. He had known Doc McCrillus for years and had previously accompanied him. He told Jim what to expect from the experience, and what he must and must not do.

"Old Doc's a tremendous fake, of course; but his heart is as big as a bucket and all pure gold. He's an optimist, never sees any but the bright side of things, and wants the folks with him to be as gay as he is himself. He won't put up with a grouch. If you try that on him, he'll pry open your mouth and dose you with one of the Remedies! He's out to have a fine time—and to garner in the coin, as he goes. I never can figure out whether he believes in his own powers as a doctor—or whether he's just a shrewd pretender. But that's of no consequence. You'll like him, I promise you! Before we've swung around this circuit you'll be swearing by him."

The McCrillus method of advertising and distribution was the same in every village visited. The handsome Buckeye would be halted on the outskirts while Mac and Jim jumped over the wheel to do some hasty but glaring lettering on fences and barns. Then the sorrels would clatter to the public square, the common, or the main street, where Doc would hold an impromptu reunion with cronies and former customers. After much handshaking, he would deliver an address on the merits of the old Remedies and read testimonials as to their efficacy; also describe in high-flown language the concoctions which he had just perfected and now was offering for the first time—and at a reduced, introductory price. Then there would be what Doc called "a bit of novelty and music," with Mac performing on the French harp and the doctor loosing a vast, mellow bass voice over the heads of his listeners.

" 'Rocked in the cradle of the dee--ee--*eep!*' " Doc would intone majestically.

Doc did not work much by day, but slept peacefully on the wagon cushions, and while he rested, the two painters scurried out to their task of plastering every available surface with advertisements and drumming up a crowd for the night's sale. If any village drugstore had purchased the Remedies, the painters would give their best efforts to

121

creating a sign which would advertise the store and its proprietor in a manner equal to Doc's own magnificence. Then, with darkness and Doc's awakening and a sumptuous meal at the hotel or restaurant (for Doc was a connoisseur of food), the sale would begin. Doc would stand in the back of the wagon; the light of kerosene flares illumining him, his great barking voice would roll forth like thunder: "Lad*eez* and gentlemen: I have here in my hand a bottle of liquid dipped from the Fountain of Perpetual Youth. Yea, verily! Are you weak, ill, disspirited? Have you chilblains, nervous headaches, stomach upsets, bad dreams, spots before the eyes? One teaspoon of this marvelous remedy, this truly miraculous mixture will make you well again. A bottle of it, taken as directed, will *lengthen your earthly life!*" . . .

By good luck, Jim had thought to bring his banjo and guitar with him, and soon he was adding his "bit of novelty and music." He played duets with Mac, and often Doc and Mac and Jim sang in trio. Sometimes Jim imitated an organ-grinder, or he wrapped the buffalo robes around Mac and bade him prowl about like a bear while Jim recited a version of his brother Humboldt's Bear Story. It was not long before Jim had become the entertainer whom the crowd demanded; his "shows," which he usually invented on the spur of the moment, were a sensation. Strumming tunes, singing, reciting, he was applauded as a master comedian.

During that summer, Jim had no chance to write poetry,

except the ludicrous little songs which he improvised for his evening's clowning, and the thought of more serious composition was almost swept from his mind. But one week, the Buckeye's destination was a town in Randolph County, near his mother's birthplace, and he went to see the bluffs of the Mississinewa River, the groves of white oaks, the site of his grandfather's cabin, where she had been a wistful, visionary little girl. As he wandered, a hundred memories stirred him: here was the stile, overgrown with trumpet vines and bittersweet, and here the meadow, a feeding ground for passenger pigeons and wild turkeys. And here were gnarled apple trees—perhaps they had been planted by Johnny Appleseed himself! All was as she had told him many times, and he seemed to feel her presence, as though she walked beside him.

That night he got his satchel out of the bottom of the wagon, took out his pads, his pencil, and for hours he wrote. The rhymes raced so fast he scarcely could snatch them back and pin them on paper; he could not hesitate to read and judge them, for fear of missing the others which jingled just behind his hurrying pencil. At dawn he put the sheaf of papers into his satchel. At some future time they must be polished and shaped and made into a poem.

With the earliest snow, Doc McCrillus wound back toward Anderson where he would winter. This was the period in which Doc worked in his "laboratory," developing next year's miraculous mixtures. There was not much for his young men to do, since they were not scientists and so could render no assistance with the Remedies. Mc-Clanahan went off to visit his parents; but Jim lingered in Anderson, renting a room in a boarding house, writing a good deal, idling about the streets, looking at people, listening to them, making the inevitable jottings and memoranda to be stuffed into the satchel.

He was quite happy. "But," he confided to Doc, "I'm broke, too. Haven't got a red cent, and my board bill's due. And I've borrowed up to the hilt of my friends' capacity to lend. So I guess I'll go home."

In February, 1873, the *Greenfield Democrat* noted the reappearance of James W. Riley. "He looks well," was the commentary which ended the item.

Chapter Twelve

ELIGHTFUL AS THE touring with Doc McCrillus had been, Jim believed in his thoughtful moments that he could better himself by a stricter application to the usual routine of sign painting. So, after the spring in Greenfield, he formed a partnership with James McClanahan. The firm was known as the Riley and McClanahan Advertising Company and on its cards, lavishly distributed, was the slogan: AD-VERTISE WITH PAINT ON BARNS AND FENCES —THAT'S THE WAY. The young men further stated that they would go anywhere at any time for any job. But now they had no luxurious Buckeye to ride in or span of horses to whisk them over the road. They traveled prosaically on trains—or (and more often) they walked. They were too restless to remain long in one town; and they became, in fact, a pair of roving gypsies.

They had some very profitable weeks, and some of dire financial embarrassment. When in funds they lived like lords; when penniless they tightened their belts and whistled for their suppers. To themselves they excused their lack of money by saying that paints and brushes cost so inordinately much. Why, it was out of all reason! They never mentioned their own extravagances. They seldom paid their debts and had been known to leave a town very suddenly, by dark, to avoid an argument with the sheriff.

Having learned from Doc McCrillus, the partners had publicity tricks in their bags. Jim would don a tall white hat, speckled trousers, a coat with gilt buttons and, carrying a cane, parade the streets, with Mac trailing behind him in overalls which had been striped to look like a convict's garb. If this did not arouse curiosity they would attire themselves as Indians, feathers in their hair, and execute a war-dance, whooping like fiends. Anything for notoriety! In the town of Peru there was the blind man farce:

Mac guided Jim into Peru, seated him in the hotel lobby, explaining to the clerk that his friend was sightless, yet an artist who could paint signs with the most marvelous accuracy. Then Mac went out to seek some local merchant who might need such service. When he returned to the hotel, a contract in his hand, he found Jim encircled

126

by commiserating folk to whom he was confiding the pitiful story of his affliction.

"If you want to see this chap at his best," Mac said, "come to the livery stable tomorrow. He's going to paint a large and beautiful picture there."

The onlookers murmured among themselves. As Mac led Jim into the restaurant, he noted from the corner of his eye how people clustered, gaping, at the door.

"They're watching, Jim."

Jim sat down at the table, dropped his napkin, fumbled for his fork, spilled the soup, upset his glass of water.

"They've fallen for it," Mac whispered softly. "If there were skeptics in the bunch—which I doubt—they're convinced. Smart boy, Jamesy, you're doing fine!"

After breakfast next morning, Jim was piloted along the street and stationed on the pavement until Mac had hoisted the ladder to the livery stable eaves. Then, with a paint bucket strapped around his waist, Jim falteringly ascended, lifted his brush.

"A little more to the left," called Mac from below. "There, that's it. Proceed!"

Jim proceeded. As extra touches of reality, he let paint dribble now and then over the bucket's lip and, when he descended at noon, he slipped and gave a nerve-racking exhibition of a man almost breaking his neck. The watchers were in a furore.

"That fellow ain't blind."

127

"Yes he is. Poor thing, poor thing! And how *brave!*"

"It isn't bravery that counts," said Mac austerely. "It's skill. Was there ever a more artistic sign painted in Peru?"

By evening the sign was finished; the crowd reluctantly dispersed, and Jim and Mac went to the hotel where they locked their door and writhed with suppressed laughter.

On the following day Mac was out scouring the town for more contracts—and securing them.

"It was a big week," they said to each other as, at the end of it, they steamed out of Peru. "A very big week—and lots of fun!"

Rain had an annoying way of interrupting their activities. When it rained for any length of time, they were reduced to foraging for their meals. They fished the brooks at the roadside and fried their catch over the red coals of camp fires. They stole into farmers' orchards and watermelon patches—and stole out again, heavily laden. They rifled corn fields for roasting ears.

"I thought I had a conscience," Mac said, "but now I know I haven't, not at least when I'm famishing."

"A man," said Jim, "must eat."

In South Bend they tarried two weeks, and here Jim achieved a masterpiece. The sign he painted was of astounding dimensions; it depicted "The Contrast of Forty Years," and was in two panels. In the first panel was Jim's conception of what South Bend must have been in 1833, a few log cabins on the St. Joe River, with an ox cart, a fur trading post and Indians in the foreground, and

128

bears and bobcats lurking in the distance. The second picture was of the modern city, stores and dwellings, a stone court house, a steamboat, and well-dressed citizens riding in Studebaker wagons.

"Gigantic!" said Jim, as he stood off to survey it. "I am proud. And I think South Benders may be surprised to know of their crude beginnings."

It was here in the northern town that Jim heard Bret Harte lecture. Since his school days he had been interested in Harte, the author of such vivid western tales as *The Luck of Roaring Camp.* Harte was a poet too and rapidly becoming famous. To Jim Riley, crouched in an inexpensive seat in the gallery, the successful author seemed the bright symbol of all which he himself hoped for. How infinitely cheering to know that Harte had struggled through a dismal period of obscurity before, at long last, he had won a thousand-dollar prize in a short story contest. Jim's pockets were at that moment crammed with scribbled verses. And what has happened once may surely happen again!

After South Bend, the Riley and McClanahan Advertising Company increased its membership to four by signing on two additional partners. The name of the organization was then changed to The Graphics. But the mode of business was not changed. Jim and Mac had merely discovered another pair of itinerant merry-makers with whom to jog about the country.

The Graphics were as roistering and madcap as young

men can be. They worked when they had to; they feasted royally; they drank—and sometimes too much. They rocketed from town to town, feeling that the world was theirs, meant solely for their delectation and pleasure. They had no fixed destination, no purpose except fun. Jim was the life of the party; the other three patterned their behavior after his and would have been content to go on so indefinitely.

But Jim, though slow to acknowledge the fact, was wearying of this vagrancy. He was, he told himself, a writer, a poet—at heart, anyway. And recently he had proved his ability. Some of his verses he had sent to the *Danbury News* in far-off Connecticut and there they had been accepted and published. The *Danbury News* was a paper with a literary flavor, and had been the stepping-stone by which many writers had climbed to eminence. The editor of the *News* had thanked Jim for his contributions and pronounced them as simple, plain, natural verses about real people and sure to charm that "average reader" of whom Jim long had thought. Such praise made Jim a bit giddy and filled him with the desire to write more worthily.

Besides, in a vague way he was homesick. His father had remarried and had bought a house on the edge of Greenfield. In the letters which Jim received from him, Mr. Riley begged his son to come back, to settle down. Mr. Riley had built a law practice again and was prospering. There would always be room for Jim, he said, in the family circle . . . "Now, my Dear Boy, come home as soon as your business will allow."

When Jim told the Graphics that he was abandoning them, they were loud in remonstrance. "But why?" they demanded. "Why?"

"I'm bored," he said truthfully.

Yet that was not quite all of it. He wanted time and solitude in which to write. And he wanted to experiment in still another direction.

One summer morning in 1874 Jim walked from Mooresville, where he had spent the night with a Marine relative, toward Monrovia, a village of four hundred inhabitants in Morgan County, Indiana. He had his paints and brushes in his hands, a guitar under his arm and a light overcoat slung across his shoulders. The hat above his sweating brow was borrowed. His face was flushed, his blue eyes glinted, and the sandy mustache which he had lately grown was waxed at the tips. The sun beat furiously upon him, dust choked him, and when presently a hack rumbled along the highway, he was glad to hail it. He gave the driver forty cents and at noon alighted in front of the little tavern in Monrovia.

After a scanty dinner, Jim ferreted out the trustees of the village. "I want to have a program here tomorrow night," he said, "Wednesday. A refined, high-class entertainment." He paused, cleared his throat and twirled his mustache. "I shall read from my own works."

131

The trustees were properly impressed and immediately said that the entertainment could be held in the meeting-house. Then Jim stalked to the tavern, painted some dodgers and several posters of announcement. On the posters he added the word COMEDIAN beneath his name, with an illustration of a fat man bent double with laughter, presumably at the comedian's witticisms. A band of children tagged after him as he went about tacking up his bills. Jim was excited and happy.

That evening, as he sat in a tilted chair at the tavern entrance, a lank and frowning man approached.

"You the fellow that's havin' the show?"

"A literary entertainment, sir," corrected Jim.

"Yeah? You stuck up these-here posters?"

"Yes, I did. Why?"

"Well, you can't use the church. The trustees didn't know you was a *comedian*. We don't want no monkeyshines there."

Jim straightened on his chair. "But I wouldn't cut monkeyshines. Heavens, no! I'll explain to the trustees—"

The man glumly shook his head. "It's settled, mister. You can't have the church." He hesitated and said. "You might get the schoolhouse, though I wouldn't bet on it."

On Wednesday morning, with some maneuvering, Jim got the schoolhouse. Then he scurried about revising the announcements and postponing the entertainment until Thursday night. He blotted out the label of COMEDIAN and, his excitement somewhat depleted, went to the tavern

132

where he tuned his guitar and rehearsed his refined program. In the afternoon he had a caller.

"You the showman goin' to do capers at the schoolhouse tomorrow night?"

"Not *capers*," protested Jim. "It's to be a very high-class—"

"Aim to sell tickets, do you?"

"There will be an admission charge, yes."

"Well, you'll have to buy a license. Two dollars."

Jim felt in his pockets. He had a dollar and no more. Sighing, he rushed out to his posters. ADMISSION FREE he scrawled on each of them.

When Thursday night came the schoolhouse was full and the town marshal was at the door. "You got the ragtag and scum of the whole neighborhood," the marshal said to Jim. "Kids, and a gang of rowdies. Shouldn't wonder if you have a scrap on your hands before you're through. Not a respectable person in the place."

Jim was sick with regret that his plans had gone so awry. But he went up on to the platform and strummed his guitar. He sang *Kathleen Mavourneen* and *The Mocking Bird*. A jumble of catcalls and hisses came from the audience. The entertainer was utterly dispirited, even frightened; but something within him, some fiber of resistance and belief in himself, would not let him stop. He gave the program just as he had mapped it, the readings from his poems, everything. Then he sat down.

In the storm of jeers and insults, a man rose. This was

the Monrovia blacksmith, an esteemed citizen, tall and bearded.

"You people have had your fun," said the blacksmith in a bellowing voice, "at this young man's expense. I think you've been right mean about it and hurt his feelings some. He's done his durndest and his show was pretty good. I move we pass the hat."

Picking up Jim's borrowed hat, the blacksmith dropped a silver piece into it and passed it through the aisle. Jim was so affected at this reversal of sentiment that tears started to his eyes. "You are—are very kind," he muttered, bowing.

Then while the shouting redoubled in violence, he saw what was in the collection. Beans, pebbles, nails and screws, buttons, a doorknob, a wad of chewing tobacco, the dried wishbone of a chicken—and forty-eight cents.

Well, he supposed that Dickens and Bret Harte must have had their hecklers, too.

Less than a year later he was on the platform again and in several Indiana towns were broadsheets:

RILEY, THE AUTHOR,
HUMORIST AND RECITATIONIST!
Will give one of his NEW AND
original Entertainments! . . .

Chapter Thirteen

THAT WAS THE year he went into his father's office. Not to study law, though Mr. Reuben Riley may have labored under the delusion that he would. Rather, Jim considered the office a quiet, sheltered place in which to write. What studying he did was of another sort: an hour or two each day he pored over text-books on rhetoric, punctuation, grammar. He had room in his mind for only one thing, the thing was poetry and with singleness of purpose he would discard everything else.

He had proof that in dedicating himself to poetry he had chosen well. His verses were being published in both the Greenfield and Indianapolis papers, and one poem had sold to *Hearth and Home,* a New York magazine with a

135

wide Midwest circulation. Jim had promptly sent a second poem on the heels of *The Dreamer:* this also, the editor said, would have been accepted but for the untimely circumstance of the magazine's going into bankruptcy.

He recalled what once he had said to his brother John, that he would not easily "beat a pathway on to wealth and fame." Indeed, the pathway was rocky and uphill; but he would not desert it. On the surface he might seem to be unsteady; underneath, his ambition was no more yielding than iron.

His father was out of the office much of the time, and this made it possible for Jim to have the solitude he craved. Ordinarily he wrote very deliberately, interlining, erasing, copying, satisfied if after a half-day one couplet rang sincerely, one stanza had a lilting meter. His poems must be *natural.* They were for the Hoosier people he knew so intimately, about small occurrences in their lives. Into this simplicity of theme no pretenses must intrude. If he wrote dialect, that must be reported with utmost accuracy.

But once Jim had an exceptional burst of inspiration. He had been writing; the title inscribed on his pad was *If I Knew What Poets Know*—and this particular poet was sure of what he wanted to say, yet could not quite bring it out. He leaned back in the swivel chair, his feet cocked on the plane of his father's ancient roll-top desk. He thrummed his pencil on his knuckles, noted how gay the morning was outside the window, how the sun sieved

through the slits in the cracked old blinds. He saw too
that his shoes needed resoling, and remembered that he
had promised his father he would attend to this item of
repair. Sighing, he threw down his pencil and pad, got up
and went to the door and out into the street, toward the
shoemaker's shop. He reached the middle of the street—
and stopped. Turning about, he retraced his steps. Now
suddenly he had the poem in mind, all of it. In the office
again, he wrote it.

> "If I knew what poets know,
>   Would I write a rhyme
>   Of the buds that never blow
>   In the summertime?
>   Would I sing of golden seeds
>   Springing up in ironweeds?
>   And of raindrops turned to snow
>   If I knew what poets know?
>
>   .   .   .
>
>   If I knew what poets know
>   I would find a theme
>   Sweeter than the placid flow
>   Of the fairest dream.
>   I would sing of love that lives
>   On the errors it forgives,
>   And the world would better grow
>   If I knew what poets know."

Jim put the manuscript into his satchel, and he had his
shoes resoled. Several days afterward he wrote *An Old
Sweetheart of Mine.* These two were by far the most sig-

nificant of his compositions to that point. Both would be printed later, and often reprinted, to win him renown.

During the summer he was sallying forth from Greenfield to Anderson, Lebanon, Crawfordsville and other small Indiana towns where he had managed to book a platform engagement. Because his clothes were so shabby and he had no money with which to buy new ones, he shunned the larger places. He would not borrow money; but when one of his friends generously provided him with a fine black broadcloth suit and a black stove-pipe hat, he boldly invaded the cities. Many people heard him; even more learned about him by means of the flaunting hand-bills which declared that: "His powers of Mimicry are free from all the strain of rant and the mock heroic. Easy, graceful, thoroughly at 'home,' he holds his throne, the rostrum and reigns SOVEREIGN OF ALL PASSIONS. Without the artifice of dress, or trickery of paint, he stands a child of five, or a tottering old man ... Cultured and refined, with a true conception of the MORAL and GOOD, he suffers no low jest or vulgar thought to desecrate his worth."

These hand-bills may have been devised by Jim himself; if so, they showed the influence of his comradeship with old Doc McCrillus.

Between engagements, and after office hours when the pads and pencils and the satchel had been put away, Jim participated in the social life of Greenfield. A few of the older residents might view him askance and lament his eccentricities, but he did not want for champions. Now that the identity of "Edyrn" and "Jay Whit" was generally known, he was regarded with admiration, too. He was not the only poet of whom Greenfield could boast—there was Captain Harris, for another; but he was the one most in the public gaze at present; and somehow the prophecy gained ground that he had a brilliant future. And he was liked for his personality. His manner was pleasant, he had the gift for making and keeping friends. As the handbills asserted, no low jests or vulgar thoughts desecrated his worth.

He was bidden to parties and lawn fetes and pie suppers, and frequently shepherded the village beaux in midnight serenades. He pounded the drums in the Adelphian Band and promoted a dramatic club known as the Adelphian Society which produced the plays of Shakespeare, Goldsmith—and Captain Harris. When Jim Riley had a role in amateur theatricals, their success was virtually a certainty.

As yet Greenfield knew little of his prowess as a platform "recitationist," for he was secretive about it. He wanted to make his reputation abroad before he displayed to the neighbors his sovereignty of ALL PASSIONS.

By degrees it was borne in upon Mr. Reuben Riley that his son was not progressing with much speed in the study of law; perhaps he was more regretful than amazed. Jim was nearly twenty-six now; his father could not dictate to him. Mr. Riley believed that the law was the best of all professions (for what was this poetry of Jim's, really?—or the "entertaining?" How could a man earn his salt at such tomfoolery?) but Mr. Riley did not upbraid him. It was blessing enough to have the boy at home, being docile and agreeable, teaching a Sunday School class, helping him with the chores and Elva May with the marketing. Mr. Riley said nothing, and hoped that no will-o'-the-wisp impulse would beckon . . .

Jim was at home all summer. Then with the perfect weather of September, the chariot of the Wizard Oil Company bowled into town behind cantering horses; and when it left, Jim Riley left also.

The Wizard Oil Company was an organization like Doc McCrillus', but on a more pretentious scale. The troupe numbered ten men, with Dr. C. M. Townsend as proprietor and conductor. Dr. Townsend sold the medicines which he had patented—Magic Oil, Sarsaparilla, Liver Pills, Cholera Balm and Cough Syrup, meanwhile staging a really stupendous concert and vaudeville show in each town through which his chariot rolled. His band was made up of trained musicians, all of whom were proficient as comedy actors. This was a medicine-man outfit of superlative proportions. If a violinist had not been discharged at Knightstown, for drunkenness, Jim probably could not have joined it.

"My lucky day!" Jim said to Dr. Townsend. "I was just getting stale, you know."

Besides substituting for the violinist, Jim was sometimes

the drummer. But his chief duty was to stand behind Dr. Townsend while he lectured and very rapidly to sketch illustrations of the talk on a huge blackboard. Dr. Townsend said he never had seen anyone who could wield the crayon at such a rate as could Jim. As fast as the words were spoken, Jim's nimble fingers flew; then having done with the illustration he would append a rhyme of his own invention, as:

> "Why let pain your pleasures spoil
> For want of Townsend's Magic Oil?"

The doctor said, too, that Jim was "no slouch at the fiddle." And Jim modestly admitted the truth of this statement.

"I would have been one of the world's great violinists," he said, "but for the fact that a door slammed on my thumb and smashed it. I would have been like Ole Bull, the great Norwegian. I heard Ole Bull once and I shall never forget it. That was in Indianapolis in 1872. Longfellow wrote a poem about him—and so will I, some day!"

"Then you're a writer, are you?"

"Oh, yes," said Jim. "I'm going to be a famous poet."

He became the doctor's confidante and a favorite with all the Wizard Troubadours. One of them was to say later, "He waded immediately boot-top deep into our affections. We laughed at his stories; everybody humored him, everybody bet on him." It seemed there was nothing he could not do, when called upon; he was so versatile—

141

cartooning with chalk, dancing, singing comic songs, im-personating—anything! Perhaps Dr. Townsend never had had a more all-round valuable employee than this Jim Riley.

The bedizened chariot shuttled north and south, and then east and west across the state, and east again, over the Ohio border. Now the travelers were in historic country, at Fort Recovery where Mad Anthony Wayne had fought; at Piqua where Tecumseh, the Indian chief had been born; at Greenville, the site of the Great Indian Treaty. Many of the Wizard company were profoundly interested and went out of their way to see such places. But Jim was provokingly indifferent. He was not interested in history. He had no sense of the past—and was never to have it, or any concern either for current national affairs, or politics or economics. Only in Upper Sandusky did he look attentively about him. Here Charles Dickens had stayed overnight, as he passed by stagecoach from Cincinnati to the Lakes. Jim wanted to see where Dickens had slept—"the large, low, ghostly room," Jim said, "with his dressing-case full of gold, gleaned from public readings!"

As the chariot went farther, Jim's wanderlust seemed to abate and he was listless, drowsy, thinking of home. He told himself that he ought to be at his writing. The weather was colder, the November days short and crisp. His companions still made much of him, but he had begun to gaze at them with lack-luster eyes. Finally, in Lima, he came to a decision, when Dr. Townsend asked him to shingle a house which the medicine man owned.

"My dear doctor, I must decline."

"But why, Jim? These are slack times. I'll pay you for the job."

"No carpentering for me, thanks."

"The fact is, you're opposed to any manual labor, Jim. Aren't you?"

"Constitutionally!"

He did consent to paint some signs for Dr. Townsend. The paintings were on glass, illuminated with verses about Magic Oil. But Jim had reached the end of his tether, and knew it.

"I'm homesick again," he said.

The *Greenfield Democrat* for December 23, 1875, carried the word of his homecoming: "James W. Riley arrived in the city on Friday last. He is looking fine and enjoying excellent health."

He was not feeling fine, though. His younger brother, Humboldt, had died. Jim had loved Humboldt, and for a long while he was disconsolate, grieving.

Chapter Fourteen

*D*URING THE FIRST months of 1876, Jim, as Jay Whit, wrote with some regularity for the newspapers of Indianapolis and smaller towns of the state, yet he had moments of bleak despair when he felt that he was at a standstill, drearily far from his goal. To be known only within a radius of forty miles from home would not suffice. He must have a broader scope!

On an October afternoon he attended a political meeting at which Robert G. Ingersoll was the speaker. The peerless orator had the national campaign as his subject, and probably he would have been astounded to learn that to Jim Riley he seemed like one sent by the gods to bring enlightenment on a totally different matter. In the course of his speech he touched upon the nobility of commonplace folk. This quality, he said, was the property of the plainest workman as well as of the most privileged aristo-

144

crat. No class or group had a monopoly on the virtues . . .
"In the lives of the people *here and now* are all of comedy
and tragedy."

"Ah!" thought Jim, listening. The statement was an
affirmation of what he himself had steadfastly believed,
not about politics—he had no concern for that—but about
poetry. If human nature was the same everywhere, a poet
who could sway his own little constricted sphere, his town,
his county, either to laughter or to tears, could reach out
to the emotions of the world at large. And this Jim would
do—or know the reason why!

The tendency then in Indiana literary circles was for
amateur authors to seek encouragement from the great.
Captain Lee O. Harris had struck up a correspondence
with John Greenleaf Whittier, and with J. T. Trowbridge
who edited a children's magazine and was the author of
books for boys. With the Captain's example before him,
Jim decided upon an audacious venture. He would write
to Longfellow!

The composition of the letter consumed many hours;
he took it to the postoffice, with tremulous hand dropped
it into the chute. At once he was beset with doubts. Had
he said anything he shouldn't have said, omitted something which shouldn't have been omitted? In the envelope
were drafts of three of his poems. But perhaps they
weren't the best, three others might have been more pleas-
ing. Perhaps in soliciting Longfellow's notice he had pre-
sumed beyond the limits of etiquette.

145

But the letter had been mailed, he couldn't snatch it back. Even so Longfellow might never receive it. Suppose he were not in Cambridge? Or ill?

"If he ever does get it, he'll probably throw it into the trash," Jim thought. "I'll never hear from him. Why should he answer me—a nobody?"

Disgruntled, he applied himself to the writing of *Fame,* a rather bitter poem which told of an artist, a sculptor, and a poet, each of whom struggled toward the realization of an ambition. They were earnest, these strivers, deserving to be smiled upon, but the Fame they craved was evasive and fickle and cruel—until too late. Artist, sculptor and poet died miserably in squalor, while Jim concluded sardonically:

> "And this is Fame! A thing, indeed,
> That only comes when least the need . . ."

He would never hear from Longfellow! Yet he haunted the postoffice. A week dragged by, ten days. Then, one morning, he was staring at a crisp white sheet of stationery which crackled in his shaking fingers.

Henry W. Longfellow had written to James W. Riley!

It was not a lengthy letter, or effusive in tone. In fact, a less eager person might have thought it quite restrained. But to Jim it seemed marvelously kind; the walls of the dingy little building seemed to fall away; he was in some enchanted land where music rippled and flowers wafted sweet perfume.

146

Hoosier Poet

The Cambridge bard said he was not in the habit of criticizing the productions of others and therefore could not discuss in detail Mr. Riley's verses. However, he would say that he had read them with a good deal of interest and judged that they indicated "the true poetic faculty and insight." His one specific criticism was that in the poem *Destiny,* Mr. Riley had misused a word. *"Prone,"* said Mr. Longfellow, "means face-downward. You meant to say *supine,* as the context shows." He was returning the pieces—"my dear Sir, with all good wishes."

According to his own phrase, Jim was "in a perfect hurricane of delight," running out of the postoffice as if his feet were winged, hugging himself, hurrying to tell Captain Harris and everyone he knew. All Greenfield shared his transports. Under the caption, "Our Poet," the *Democrat* printed the Longfellow letter with pertinent observations on the achievements of "our young fellow townsman, James W. Riley . . .

"We are gratified to learn that his poetic talent has not only been appreciated by his friends at home, but has received the recognition of America's most eminent poet. The *Democrat* is proud of having one among us whose brilliant future is almost assured . . ."

For a while Jim basked in this glow; he was a hero, congratulated on every side. If ever he had wavered in his will to write, he knew now that he *must,* that writing was to be his life's work.

It was a foolish mistake to make, though, not to know

the exact definitions of *supine* and *prone*. He blushed, thinking of it and swore never to commit another such blunder. Henceforth he would choose his words with scrupulous care.

He began immediately to put together *The Funny Little Fellow,* a "serio-humorous" poem which he illustrated with several drawings. He sent it to *Scribner's,* and was somehow positive that it would be taken there. When it was declined, Jim gritted his teeth. He'd storm and vanquish those coolly superior eastern editors! This fellow out "in the sticks" was not to be so cavalierly dealt with! Hadn't he Longfellow's letter in his pocket? With that, how could he fail? He bombarded the magazines with his manuscripts—

Like so many crows, they all came back to him! He moped, he sulked and thought of himself as the counterpart of the poet in his own mournful *Fame.* He seemed to have tobogganed from the pinnacle of promise into the depths of disillusionment.

Once he had said to his partner, McClanahan, that a man must eat; now he was reminded of the sad yet unescapable fact. Without money or a job, with platform engagements few and far between, he faced a financial crisis. He had supposed that by writing poetry he could live; but the essential necessity, as he now saw it, was to live that he might write poetry.

And so, in April, 1877, he went to Anderson, to a berth on the weekly *Democrat* there. His salary was to be forty dollars a month, which seemed a princely sum, since it was twice as much as ever he'd made before.

Mr. Todisman and Mr. Croan, owners of the *Anderson Democrat,* saluted with fanfare the addition to their staff. In a front page placard they said that his poems already had attracted the scrutiny of such men as Longfellow, Whittier, Trowbridge and other celebrities. "We believe we not only benefit ourselves and patrons by the acquisition of his services, but that he is also supplied with a congenial position, and one in which he will develop the highest attributes of his nature."

Exchange newspapers had similar tributes to bestow. According to the *Indianapolis Herald,* J. W. Riley was "one of the best writers among the young litterateurs of the west." From all around the state came good wishes that he would "find many roses" in his pathway, that the *Democrat* would "grow under the spell of his versatile genius."

It was good, Jim thought, to be so greeted; he would do his best. He said that while his position was one "fraught with a thousand trials and vexations," he would not be deterred from "the steadfast purpose of right and justice." His first contribution was a burlesque of Maud Muller; he said it was meant as "a mere bagatelle," yet it provoked mirth wherever it was read.

He might speak solemnly of his duties; in reality they were not of an exalted sort. He was a reporter who doubled as an editor of the news items brought or sent to the *Democrat* from rural contributors. These items he must rewrite. In doing so he sometimes embellished them to such a degree that the original scribes would never have known them. His copy was always humorous, an extraordinary amount of it in rhyme. Even his prose was decked with florid phrases, and his verse bubbled up in such volume that it threatened to inundate the paper. The *Democrat* took on an odd and distinctive look, and readers were at a loss to know when some straightforward, informative news story might suddenly taper off into a final rhymed couplet.

This propensity to make verses of everything Jim carried over into the advertising columns. Why not brighten up the advertising? Mr. Todisman had no objections, and Jim began an "idyl on business," in which he touted categorically the wares sold in each of the Anderson shops and stores. "The huge appetite of the public for wonders," he said, "requires daily food." And he would supply it.

The idyl swung into print with a salute to the hardware merchant and went on from there, indefatigably.

> " 'What boots it?' Shakespeare asks—
> We answer Conwell's Store;
> For never boots were better made,
> Or sold as cheaply to the trade
> In Anderson before."

He neglected none of the advertisers, not even the proprietor of the repair shop where a farm wagon's splintered

150

single-tree could be mended. Jim was very thoughtful of
the farmers. "Ye men of the streets," he entreated, "be
cordial to our rustic brethren. Do all you can for them.
Farmers should vibrate wisely between the Public Square
and the farm—and *we* of the town should do the same."

The agent who sold sewing machines was another person whom Jim considered as a benefactor. "The drudgery
of millions of poor women is at an end," he said:

> "Backward, throw backward the curtain tonight,
> Open the window and let the glad light
> Of the round moon shimmer over the scene
> Where we at last own a sewing machine."

He wrote about the bank, too; the "shaving parlor,"
the jail:

> "Give us the log jail with two rooms interfused,
> No friends but the darkness, no windows to loot,
> The old-fashioned jail that our grandfathers used."

To the readers in smaller, outlying villages he said:

> "Could I pour out the nectar the gods only can,
> I would fill up my glass to the brim
> And drink the success of the Suburban Man."

The collecting of material for this idyl entailed prodigious time and work, but Jim was indomitable, once he

151

had started. His knack of soaking up impressions was such that he could glance for only a minute down the shelves at the grocer's, and then have in memory every commodity ranged there. As he went alertly along the streets, through the alleys, he became known as the Perspiring Poet. Anderson was fond of him, hilariously so, laughing at him and with him. To borrow Jim's own words, he was "running round the country like a waterbug"; "a perfect nebula of new subscribers bespangled" the Todisman and Croan list.

> "The lark is up to meet the sun,
> The bee is on the wing;
> The Democrat it has begun
> To go like everything."

He wrote many more serious poems; these also were published in the paper. He had a little room: "No. 19—North Main Street—Up Stairs—In the Rear," where he scribbled at night. His satchel was now too small to hold the stanzas he wrote, revised, toiled over; he got a collapsible leatherette "telescope," and then a trunk. His rule, from which he was never to deviate, was to destroy nothing. The scraps must all be kept, against the day when he should be famous. He spoke of himself as "the little bench-leg poet," but his dreams were tremendous and rosy. He was nearing a climax significant to his work.

152

Chapter Fifteen

ONE MIDSUMMER EVENING Jim lounged
with several of his friends just outside the
Anderson hotel. It was a group that often assembled there in tilted-back chairs, smoking and chatting
—Mr. Croan, Jim's editor; Samuel Richards, a cartoonist;
Captain W. R. Myers, a Civil War veteran; James Mc-
Clanahan, Jim's pal of the old Graphic days who now was
a law clerk; and William Kinnaird, the editor of the
Herald, which was the *Democrat's* rival journal. They
knew each other well, these six. They liked to talk together, and to quibble.

"Jim," Mr. Kinnaird said, baitingly, "I hear you've
been hurling your poems eastward—and getting 'em back
so fast that your head swims."

Jim smiled. "There's some truth in that."

"Why don't you quit pushing your pen around and go to sign-painting?"

"Kinnaird wishes you would, Riley," said Mr. Croan, "for he can't compete with you as a newspaper man."

"I'm not accepted by the magazine because I'm just a Hoosier hick with no reputation—as yet."

"Is a reputation important?" Kinnaird queried.

"*Is* it? Above everything else! The manuscript doesn't matter much, if only the author has a name."

Captain Myers, a man of education and culture, broke in: "Wrong, Jim! You're the typical young writer, justifying your failures by charging that the publishers are short-sighted and stubborn."

"They are short-sighted," Jim said. "And stubborn. Very."

"No, no!" Captain Myers shook his head. "Merit is what counts. Just merit. Why, this song, *Paddle Your Own Canoe,* it's sung everywhere, as much in New England as in the Middle West, sung even in Europe—and who, except ourselves here in Indiana, knows that it was written by Sarah T. Bolton, a Hoosier?"

"If the signature on the song had been Longfellow's, its popularity would have been instantaneous," Jim said, "and considerably greater. Merit, indeed! A few years ago Henry Ward Beecher was paid twenty-five thousand dollars by the *New York Ledger* for a manuscript which, without Beecher's name, would have landed smack in the waste basket."

"And what about Longfellow's *Hanging of the Crane?*" said McClanahan. "Three thousand dollars for that! If I'd written it, I wouldn't have got thirty dollars!"

"Or thirty cents," said Jim. "You'd have got a rejection slip, Mac."

Captain Myers puffed at his pipe. "You contend, do you, that the beginner doesn't have a fair chance?"

"That's what I say—and think."

"I dispute it! Nothing can keep real genius down. It will hurdle all barriers and rise. Rise!" Captain Myers made a sweeping gesture. "Yes, sir!"

"But a poem over the signature of Bryant, Whittier, Tennyson would have the preference in a magazine editor's office over the work of some unknown like—well, like me, Captain."

"I think not," said Captain Myers.

"Not a bit of it!" exclaimed Kinnaird. "If your work were the equal of Tennyson's—"

"It is!" said McClanahan. "Or almost, anyway."

"But Jim himself admits that he's inferior to the really great. Don't you, Jim?" Kinnaird taunted.

"I'll not admit anything." Jim still smiled, though now he had flushed. "I'd be interested in seeing the comparison made between a poet with a bona-fide reputation and me. That might amaze you, gentlemen."

Captain Myers chuckled. "No, no! Merit is what counts, my boy."

"Improve your stuff, Riley," said Kinnaird, getting up, "and you'll find your eastern market."

Jim was spending the night with Mac and they strolled to his boarding-house beneath a mellow July moon. Mac went to bed; but Jim, sleepless, sat in his nightshirt at the window, remembering the Captain's insistence upon merit as the one sure means of winning literary spurs, and Kinnaird's sly thrusts at Riley's "stuff." Jim felt that it wasn't he who had been wrong in the altercation.

"No," he murmured, "I'm *right*. I do have talent equal to some of the best. I could write a poem which no author, living or dead, need be ashamed of! If I wanted to, I could show Kinnaird!"

He leaned on the sill, looking out at the lawn, the hushed street. He was thinking of a rhyme, an air, a theme.

"Leonainie—angels named her"; . . .

For a week the lovely name of Leonainie had been in his mind. It was a word like a purling brook, melodious, flowing, a name which would have intrigued Edgar Allan Poe. With such a name to inspire him, what wonders Poe could have wrought. And Jim Riley could do as well! Hadn't he always been impressed with the rhythmic beauty of Poe's meter, his romantic melancholy? Why, just recently Jim had parodied *The Bells*. In an advertisement written for the Bell Brothers, Anderson dry-goods merchants, he had caught Poe's manner.

156

"Leonainie—angels named her;
And they took the light
Of the laughing stars and framed her
In a smile of white . . ."

There, that was quite like Poe! With concentration, Jim could go on, writing a poem so exactly in Poe's style that its authenticity never would be questioned.

Suppose he tried it? What fun, to fool Captain Myers and old Kinnaird! Other people, too! A literary ruse?

Why not?

Jim got to his feet, paused; then he fetched a pencil and paper from his coat which was hung over a chair-back. Mac was snoring fearsomely and Jim would not disturb him with the lamp. But he could see, anyway; the moon silvered the window ledge. And this would be only a first rough draft . . .

He didn't change that first draft much; he dared not; for *Leonainie* seemed to have come to him magically out of the dew-scented, moon-drenched summer night. In the morning he told Mac about it, and they laughed gleefully. During the next day or two he told four more bosom friends. All were sworn to secrecy. Samuel Richards said that the faking would be more fun than a barrel of monkeys and he hoped he might have a hand in it.

"If I can help as you go along, Jim," said Richards, "just holler."

With the verses completed, Jim had misgivings. But

they were good, and to publish them would be only a joke —which he could explain later.

Obviously *Leonainie* mustn't be printed in the *Democrat*. Anderson knew the Perspiring Poet pretty well by this time; he would be suspected. Jim cast about for some other paper in Indiana which might be a suitable vehicle. In Kokomo there was that John Henderson fellow, editor of the *Dispatch*. Jim didn't know Henderson, but recently he'd had a letter from him, in which Henderson alluded to "the gifted J. W. Riley." Evidently a man of perception!—and Kokomo was just the proper distance away.

Jim wrote to Henderson, asking "a rather curious favor." The dull times worried him, Jim said; he would like to "stir things from their comatose condition." Perhaps Mr. Henderson would be inclined to assist in the stirring process—by printing in the *Dispatch* a poem which would be an imitation of "some popular American poet, deceased," and so excellent an imitation that the gullible public would believe in it until the moment came for Jim to "bu'st our literary balloon."

As to the method of presentation, that was left to Mr. Henderson to choose. Jim suggested experimentally that it might be said "the *original manuscript* was found in the album of an old lady living in your town—and in the handwriting of the poet imitated—together with signature, etc., etc. . . ." But this was just an idea; Mr. Henderson could fix the prefacing story as he deemed best. "Only," begged Jim, "be sure to *clinch* it so as to defy the scrutiny of the most critical lens. Should you fall in with the plan, write me . . ."

Mr. Henderson fell in. "Yes, my dear Riley, I am with you, boots and soul." Jim grinned, perusing that response; Henderson thought the plan a capital one, most cunning, a journalistic scoop! He said that he understood everything which Jim implied. "I assure you that I tumble to it . . . But," he asked, "hadn't I better forestall the poem by a 'startling announcement' or something of the sort one week before its publication?"

A variety of startling announcements were scanned during the ensuing two weeks. *Leonainie* might be the discovery of "an aged washerwoman," or of a wood-sawyer; it might have been unearthed by a hunter refuging in a hillside cave from a thunderstorm. A dwarf might have had it, or a hermit. Henderson had said that "Mum's the word!" but, perplexed, he took into his confidence one friend, a Kokomo butcher. Jim himself was rather less discreet. Somehow thirteen people had now edged into the secret. The thing was so irresistibly funny that Jim scarcely could forbear from shouting it in the Anderson streets.

Out of Henderson's conference with the butcher evolved what all the conspirators thought a credible, though exciting, story. Meanwhile Jim had forwarded his poem and been assured that it was "a rare and marvelous creation, honoring you and the State as well," a verdict with which the creator was quite in accord.

159

Then, on August 2, 1877, the *Dispatch* was ready with its broadside:

POSTHUMOUS POETRY

A Hitherto Unpublished Poem of the Lamented Edgar
Allan Poe—Written on the Fly Leaf of an Old
Book Now in Possession of a Gentleman of
This City.

In glowing terms the article related the discovery of the beautiful posthumous poem from the pen of the erratic Poe:

"Calling at the house of a gentleman of this city the other day, on a business errand, our attention was directed to a poem written on the blank fly leaf of an old book. Handing us the book, he observed that it (the poem) might be good enough to publish . . . Noticing the initials, E. A. P., at the bottom of the poem, it struck us that possibly we had run across a 'bonanza,' so to speak, and after reading it, we asked who its author was . . ."

The old gentleman had thereupon indulged in a bit of reminiscence for the benefit of the *Dispatch* reporter. He did not, alas, know just who was the author. He himself never had seen him; but the old gentleman's grandfather who, long ago, had owned the book, had told of the circumstances in which the poem had been written.

This patriarch had been the keeper of a country hotel, a wayside inn, in the village of Chesterfield, near Richmond, Virginia. One night a young man, plainly the worse for

160

extreme dissipation, had rapped at the inn door and demanded a bed, and had been accommodated. But next morning, the room in which the pallid young man had slept was empty. Before dawn the guest had gone, never to be glimpsed again, and leaving behind him a book, on the fly leaf of which were written the lines of a poem.

"Further than this," said the *Dispatch,* "our informant knows nothing, and being an uneducated, illiterate man, it was quite natural that he should allow the great literary treasure to go for so many years unpublished . . .

"The poem is written in Roman characters, and is almost as legible as print itself, although somewhat faded by the lapse of time." The *Dispatch* was willing to swear that its statement was true and the revealing of it "no canard," and would take pleasure in satisfying anyone who cared to investigate.

Therewith, *Leonainie* was reproduced:

"Leonainie—angels named her;
  And they took the light
Of the laughing stars and framed her
  In a smile of white;
    And they made her hair of gloomy
    Midnight, and her eyes of bloomy
    Moonshine, and they brought her to me
    In the silent night.

In a solemn night of summer,
  When my heart of gloom

161

Blossomed up to greet the comer
  Like a rose in bloom;
    All forebodings that distressed me
    I forgot as joy caressed me—
    Lying joy that caught and pressed me
    In the arms of doom! . . .

Then God smiled and it was morning.
  Matchless and supreme;
Heaven's glory seemed adorning
  Earth with its esteem;
    Every heart but mine seemed gifted
    With the voice of prayer, and lifted
    Where my Leonainie drifted
    From me like a dream."

Jim had been anxiously waiting and now he was charmed. "Dear, *dear* Henderson," he wrote, "and I have a notion to call you darling, The introduction is superb. As for the leading paragraph, a neater, sweeter lie was never uttered . . . Let no one know it—not even your *mother-in-law* . . . In the language of Artemus Ward— 'I am here—I think so—Even of those.' "

Henderson was not, it seemed, a person for half-measures. Having resurrected *Leonainie,* he reprinted it on cards which he mailed to newspapers and magazines in every state in the Union. With each card was the entreaty that it be published and credit given to the *Kokomo Dispatch.*

The poem was a torpedo sundering the complacence of
162

the reading public. Scarcely was the ink dry on Henderson's press before inquiries barraged him. Was this an authentic thing or merely a forgery? Newspapers in New York, Chicago, Philadelphia, Brooklyn, Cincinnati, Baltimore, Nashville debated, with the forgery premise having the larger vote. "The poem bears no internal evidence of Poe's paternity." . . . "If that gentleman ever wanders anywhere in spirit, he will surely pay his respects to the scalp of the Indiana man that wrote it." . . . "The story is lurid enough to have been written under the influence of Egyptian whiskey." . . . "Poe was doubtless guilty of many indiscretions, but it is hard to suppose that in his most eccentric moods he would have attempted to foster *Leonainie*. It is a libel to hint of such doleful idiocy." . . .

Probably nothing ever before printed in a country weekly had so involved the nation in controversy. And Jim Riley in Anderson rocked with laughter. He had made "the big dailies stand on their heads and bark furiously," which was all he had hoped for. He too, joined the parley, reviewing the poem in his own columns and saying that after grave thought, he could neither affirm nor deny its authenticity. *Leonainie* had its faults, yes; but in the main it was an exhibition of Poe's "weird faculty of attractively combining with the delicate and beautiful, the dread and repulsive—a power most rarely manifest, and quite beyond the bounds of imitation."

To Henderson he wrote privately: "God bless us, we are certainly at the very threshold of success. Hold the

163

fort! If we could talk for one square hour we could make *ourselves* believe it."

When discussion raged most fiercely, Mr. Henderson encountered a tangle not premeditated. In Boston a man who was Poe's biographer asked that the manuscript be sent to him. As one familiar with Poe's handwriting, the Bostonian could settle the matter.

Somewhat dismayed, Henderson referred this problem to Jim—who "hollered" for Samuel Richards. The cartoonist leaped into the breach, copying the lines on the fly leaf of an ancient *Ainsworth's Dictionary* and doing it with detail and skill. Then Jim swathed the book in brown paper and boarded the train for Kokomo.

It was the first meeting between the conspirators. Henderson was alone in his office that warm evening when the door was opened by a shabbily-dressed, sandy-mustached fellow whose smile was furtive and yet jovial.

"Are you the editor?"

"Yes, sir. What can I do for you?"

"I'm Riley."

"No! I thought you'd be an older man!" Henderson grasped the poet's hand. "You don't look much like a writer."

"Maybe not."

"I thought you'd have curly hair and dimples."

Jim shrugged. "I've brought you the *Leonainie* manuscript." He laid his parcel on the desk and watched while Henderson inspected it. "Rather clever, isn't it?"

164

"Fine!" said Henderson. "I've been worried crazy because of this biographer popping up."

"Oh, you mustn't worry," Jim said. "Things are moving swimmingly. I guess you haven't told anybody?"

"Only people I can trust."

"That's been my policy," Jim said. "You just sit tight here. I'm going for a few days' rest in Greenfield."

Henderson deposited the *Ainsworth's Dictionary* in a drawer. "Under double lock and key, Riley! Let the Boston chap yelp now, eh? And mum's still the word?"

"Mum it is!" said Jim.

But things were moving at a faster pace than these two realized, and James McClanahan was assailed by some erratic whim of conscience. Mac had been Jim Riley's closest friend for years, yet even as Jim rested in his father's home in Greenfield, Mac, in an Anderson restaurant, was talking very earnestly to Kinnaird of the *Herald*.

"It seems to me," Mac said, "that the time has come for the *Leonainie* bubble to burst."

"Then it *is* Riley's!" ejaculated Kinnaird. "I thought so!"

"Yes. I feel I ought to tell you."

"Thanks, Mac." Kinnaird clapped McClanahan's shoulder. "Of course, you ought! A civic duty! Well, the Perspiring Poet has had his little scoop. Now I'll have mine!"

Mac sighed. "I guess by tomorrow morning the secret will be walking up and down the streets."

"And it should be!" said Kinnaird.

Yet, for some unplumbed reason, Kinnaird hesitated; and in the interval, Mr. Croan, Jim's editor on the *Democrat,* dashed off a message to Greenfield. "The *Herald* has just got wind of it and swears it will expose the entire thing . . . I write you as a friend warning you of the danger." Reading that warning, Jim was dizzy, breathless. How and why should McClanahan have been so unfaithful! And what was to be done to parry the blow?

There was nothing to be done. At the last moment, Kinnaird's soft heart would not permit him to spring the trap himself. After all, he liked Jim and would not antagonize him—at least, not too directly. Though Kinnaird had derided the Hoosier poet, he had a sneaking premonition that perhaps some day Jim might amount to something. Therefore, Kinnaird was content to retail the thrilling tale of the Poe ruse to a neighbor, the editor of the *Kokomo Tribune,* who would be very glad to embarrass both Jim and Henderson, as well. Kinnaird could sit back and witness the explosion.

It happened with a noise and turbulence for which Jim was totally unprepared. He had thought, when launching *Leonainie,* that it was only a small venture, a bit of nonsense, that could be easily explained and smoothed over. But publicity had been much too wide-spread and far-reaching for such a denouement. The ruse had proved to be a volcano, abruptly erupting and loosing upon Jim a flood of scalding, searing denunciation. Every newspaper, magazine and critic's journal which had printed the poem now took to task its author. He was "a fraud," "an un-scrupulous villain"; he was not a poet, never had been or would be; he was guilty of "an exceedingly foolish piece of criminality," and henceforth there would ever be "an impassable gulf" between Riley and fame. "A brilliant career has been lost to the literary world."

In Kokomo, Henderson valiantly tried to exonerate Jim. The publishing of *Leonainie* had been meant only as an innocent prank. The poem was a good one—had any other ever been so quoted by the American press? Of course, the story which prefaced it was fiction; but Henderson, not Riley, was responsible for that.

"Mr. Riley is a young poet of great promise," main-tained Henderson in the *Dispatch*, "and will yet make his mark as one of the sweetest singers of the age."

Jim needed such comfort, for he was stunned. He be-lieved what the newspapers were saying, that his career was at an end, he was utterly ruined. He could not go back to Anderson, yet to linger in Greenfield was torture. He neither ate nor slept; he skulked indoors, feeling that if he went out, his friends would refuse to speak to him. In the depths of dejection he drank to drown his sorrow and then, knowing how futile was this weakness, he vowed he would never drink again. At night or in the early morning, when no one could see, he tramped out of town to the Brandywine, trudged up and down along its banks, morose and penitent.

There, finally, he thought of something which might

167

extricate him from his Slough of Despond. A public apology . . .

On August 30, 1877, the *Indianapolis Journal* published his "Card to the Public." It was a clarification of the "alleged Poe-poem" ruse, from start to finish, with Jim confessing his authorship of *Leonainie,* his regret that he had been placed in a false light. In closing, he asked pardon for those of his friends who had been good enough to help him and begged that he himself be held "blameless of all dishonorable motives." He was, he said, "Yours truly, J. W. Riley."

Gradually, after that, he realized that he had exaggerated his plight. Greenfield hadn't ostracized him; Indiana was faithful to him. Let other people rave and berate, he was the bard of the Hoosier homefolks. They would forget his little escapade—and there was nothing to forgive. They knew Jim; he had intended no harm. He was theirs, and they threw their love like a protective blanket around him.

Chapter Sixteen

H E WAS WRITING once more, in a tiny room on the shady side of Main Street, which he rented by the month—working so diligently that when some roistering companion of other days would stop and tempt him with the mention of fun to be found elsewhere, Jim would reply:

"No time! I have to stay in this small, cozy Morgue of mine and sew my shroud. You trot along and sell your chestnuts. I'll woo the Muse."

Often he wrote for hours at a stretch. He had notes all over the table, under it, under the lamp, in his hat and shoes, and so voluminously in his umbrella that when he raised it, the slips deluged him like a pelting of snow-flakes.

In his father's house, up under the cupola, he had a

second retreat; he dubbed it the Crow's Nest, a starkly bare chamber, dirty and littered, with one uncurtained window. But whether there or in the Morgue, he was as withdrawn from the world as any monk. He had meager concern for sleeping and only thought of eating when Mary, his younger sister, forced food upon him.

"Now, Jim," Mary would admonish, "you can't starve yourself so. Elva May and I won't have it! We've baked this cake for you and I shall see that you swallow every bite of it."

His poems were being published in newspapers throughout the country in 1878; and he was lecturing. At first, in reviving it, he had been timid lest the *Leonainie* episode should harass him. But when in February, just five months after the exposure of the hoax, he was asked to speak in Kokomo, the very place which had witnessed his humiliation, he knew that *Leonainie* was a thing of the past, never again to plague him. After Kokomo, he went to other towns; his fee was five dollars, advancing to fifteen, then to twenty-five.

It had been his custom to draw material for his programs ("my argying," he called it) from many sources, to interpret the poems of Longfellow and Burns, and of lesser writers. These he would intersperse with his own poems, though he concealed that fact by saying shyly: "Here's a little thing which may please. Clipped it from a magazine. I don't know exactly who *did* write it, but it has a nice sound." Often enough his audience would smile, knowing who had written it. The "little things" were quite likely to be the best of Jim's selections, recited with real artistry.

Occasionally, and perhaps inevitably, he made mistakes in gauging the reactions of his hearers. He had in his personality a vein of the morbid and, by contrast, a tendency toward satire, neither of which was especially suitable to a performance before a crowd. But he had also an eagle eye for frowns upon the countenances out in front; he was quick to perceive if he had offended, he seldom repeated a mistake.

The burlesque of Robert Ingersoll and the ludicrous sketch of Luther Benson, Indiana's temperance leader, were ruled out by this trial and error system. They were unpopular, and so they must go into the discard. Not then or at any time in his life was there a trace of harshness in his disposition. He was courteous, considerate, wanting the men and women, the children, who listened to him to be as fond of him as he was honestly fond of them.

He had always been an able actor; and acting was precisely what his "argying" became; there could be no other term for it. Though he had qualms of nervousness before facing his audience, once there, he was serene, forgetting everything except the story he had to tell, the poem, going from one role to the next, portraying an aged farmer, a pompous teacher, an itinerant "hired man," or a lisping little waif, and being for the moment each of these persons. He sank himself in the character he assumed; even his appearance altered, the illusion was matchless, perfect.

As the months wore on and his audiences were always so responsive, Jim read more and more from his own poems and was not so reluctant to acknowledge them.

Much of this verse was in dialect, for he had a genuine enthusiasm for the quaint, slurred speech of the rural Hoosier. The people who spoke dialect were, Jim said, very near to his heart and "as capable of heroism as college men or ladies of fashion." No one could attack dialect without his springing to its defense. Grammarians, he declared, were "not the only ones made in the image of God!"

He believed that every normal human being, whether young or old, loved poetry and cherished a sense of the beautiful; but he contended that the "average person" must be talked to in an unaffected style and language, about things within his experience. If poetry did not appeal, the fault was not with the people to whom it was addressed, but with the poet.

Lecturing or writing, Jim thought of this "average person," and saw him not with condescension but rather with admiration, as a simple, earthy sort of creature, liking pathos and broad humor, having only a scant background of culture and none too much intelligence. There might be those who would dispute Jim's picture and say it was untrue to life; but he held tenaciously to it. For such a man or woman, the typical Hoosier, Jim had a philosophy, his own:

172

"They's been a heap o' rain, but the sun's out today,
  And the clouds of the wet spell is all cleared away,
  And the woods is all the greener, and the grass is greener
      still;
  It may rain again to-morry, but I don't think it will.
  Some says the crops is ruined, and the corn's drownded out,
  And propha-sy the wheat will be a failure, without doubt;
  But the kind Providence that has never failed us yet,
  Will be on hands onc't more at the 'leventh hour, I bet! . . .

"Then let us one and all, be contented with our lot;
  The June is here this morning, and the sun is shining hot.
  Oh! let us fill our harts up with the glory of the day,
  And banish ev'ry doubt and care and sorrow far away!
  Whatever be our station, with Providence fer guide,
  Such fine circumstances ort to make us satisfied;
  Fer the world is full of roses, and the roses full of dew,
  And the dew is full of heavenly love that drips fer me and
      you."

In March, 1879, Jim took part in an entertainment promoted by the foremost musicians and literary leaders of
Indianapolis. It was his first formal appearance there, and
was to have consequences. At the time, he only knew that
he had attempted to do justice to himself and his verses
and that he seemed to have been moderately successful.

He had recently sold some poems to the *Journal,* and he
collected the money due him. As he ambled in the shop-
ping district he felt blithe and stimulated. Spying a red
silk hat in a store window, he went in and bought it. The

color was a challenge; a modish hat; but, more than that, it seemed to Jim an emblem.

"I'm getting on," he thought. "I really am, you know." And tapping the crimson crown to a rakish slant, he hurried to catch his train and ride back in splendor to Greenfield.

He seldom wore the hat, but he stowed it in the Morgue where he could gaze at it and grin, as if at his own impudence. He was in jocund mood just then, anyway, for he was up to mischief of the brand he most relished, a bit of sly waggery.

It had to do with writing, of course. Poems were being printed in the *Kokomo Tribune,* signed John C. Walker, and many subscribers had been struck by the likeness of Mr. Walker's work to that of James Whitcomb Riley.

"John C. Walker," said one Indiana editor, "has much of the peculiar flavor of Riley, and is certainly destined to divide honors with him."

He had been "Edyrn" and "Jay Whit"—and Poe, also, briefly; though this thought he put behind him. Now with a new pen name he lurked in his hideaway and chuckled.

He hadn't yet sold a single manuscript to a magazine; it was not for lack of trying. But he would, he said to himself. "I'll crack that wall of smug prejudice, no matter how long I have to hammer at it!"

Meanwhile, his local fame grew apace, and in September he had a letter from General Daniel Macauley of Indianapolis. Why not a public testimonial benefit for the Hoosier poet in the state capital? General Macauley would arrange it, if Jim liked the idea.

He liked it, immensely, and he communicated his feeling to the General, who was a man of much prestige in the city.

The theater was at once secured and the date fixed. Jim said that he had no money—

"Dear Boy," answered General Macauley by the next mail, "You don't need one cent—don't think of it. We will do *everything* and if there is profit it is yours—if not it is *ours*. We esteem it a privilege . . . The public is a capricious beast and may have some d—d fool engagement that night elsewhere, but propose to give them an all-fired good chance to 'come and see us.' You have . . . nothing more to do with it but to speak your piece and 'collar the boodle' afterwards. We blow out in the *Herald* this week, and then fire all along the line."

Ever since the March entertainment, General Macauley had been saying that Riley was "the greatest bard south of 54:40." Now he added a clause to the assertion: "And I'll *prove* it."

Jim was flattered, and apprehensive. The burden of proof would be upon him. He mustn't disappoint!

"An humming like a telegraph pole," he wrote. "Chrlpkin aprrrrooommmm!!! Yours gaspingly, J. W. R."

The *Herald* "blew out" in very black headlines:

175

NEW PARK THEATER
Thursday Evening, October 16 (1879)
Complimentary Testimonial to
MR. J. W. RILEY
THE INDIANA POET
Tendered by the citizens of Indianapolis
An Evening of Original Character
Sketches and Dialectic Readings

Jim was awed; suspense seized upon him. This was an ordeal with much at stake. General Macauley had imposed a trust and predicted that he would be a "howling hit." But suppose he wasn't? Now he would not be one number on a program, a few minutes of diversion. He was to be the whole show, "the shebang," as General Macauley was saying. He thought over his repertory and questioned which poems would be most likely to please the sophisticated people of the city.

Soon he was informed that there would, indeed, be other lures for the public, on the night of October sixteenth—a circus, a minstrel show; and the lovely young actress Mary Anderson, playing in *Evadne*. Jim groaned. How could he win an audience against such competition? In imagination he saw the throngs wending toward the circus, the minstrels, and Mary Anderson—and at the Indiana Poet's benefit, only himself stranded on a garishly lighted stage below empty, echoing galleries reciting to General Macauley, solitary and bereft in the yawning pit.

176

His restiveness increased with each day; isolation in the Crow's Nest or the Morgue augmented the fear that he would fail his sponsor. A week before the lecture date he decided abruptly to go to Indianapolis. His brother John was living there, and Uncle Mart, too. Perhaps they would take him under their wings and help him to wait more patiently for what he now thought of as his "undoing."

He told his father that he had to buy sleeve buttons and shoe strings and have his "justly celebrated complexion powdered," and that these operations would require time. Then, kissing his sisters and wringing his father's hand, he set out.

"I shall have a week," he said, "in which to ramble— and to worry."

Jim was no stranger to Indianapolis; he had frequently visited there. But probably he never before had so deviously explored it. In 1879 it was a city of approximately 70,000 inhabitants, originally bounded by the "mile-square," but rapidly pushing beyond that, northward toward Fall Creek and the old Canal, eastward and south into the farm regions. To an extent it retained the look of a large, sprawling town. Streets were paved with cobblestones for the most part, a few were made of cedar blocks; sidewalks were uneven, either of brick or planks, without uniformity. Houses were big and comfortable-looking, framed by well-tended gardens, fringed by elms and maples and beeches. Even then Indianapolis had developed that aspect which it was to keep always, of being a community of solid, prosperous, home-loving people, neither extremely rich nor noticeably poor, an air of stanch, self-respecting independence, of self-sufficiency, which would lend it individuality and distinction among all the cities of America.

In the center of what had been the "mile-square" was the Circle, a round area of trees and grass plot, girdled by a low white fence; from this the streets radiated out like the spokes of a wheel to the compass points—a device borrowed from the national Capital at Washington, which had been planned and executed by Pierre L'Enfant, under the supervision of George Washington. Indianapolis was proud of its Circle and was glancing toward the time when it should be properly ornamented, perhaps with a monument erected to immortalize the state's heroic soldier dead. At one intersection of the Circle stood Christ Church, which was a perfect gem of Gothic ecclesiastical architecture; here also, a bit farther on, were the homes of Bishop Talbot and of William H. English, the Indiana historian, and the house which, some years before, had sheltered Henry Ward Beecher, when he was a young man, preaching to his Indianapolis congregation.

Along the downtown streets mule-cars trundled at regular intervals, though they could be stopped and boarded anywhere, at any signal from a passenger. The drivers of the mules perched precariously on tiny elevations at the front of the cars and were most mannerly and accommodating fellows, willing to pause while a passenger dis-

178

mounted and ran into a shop on some urgent errand, and then drive on again. The fare charged was five cents for adults; children rode free; but behind each conductor was posted a conspicuous announcement that wash baskets would be carried only if the space they took up was paid for; a small wash basket was taxed five cents; a large one, a dime. On many corners in the business section were pumps, hung with tin cups and dippers, where the thirst of pedestrians could be assuaged; and under striped awnings were numerous outdoor fruit-stands which offered for sale such tropical delicacies as oranges, bananas and pineapples. Up and down the streets, bootblacks plied their trade and newsboys scurried. Bookshops abounded, for Indianapolis was a city of readers; more than a score of citizens could boast of fine and costly private libraries, and the public library was a mecca for students. "Magazine Day" each month was a day of importance, for then it was that *Harpers* and the *Century* and the *Atlantic* arrived by train and were distributed from the bookshops. From early morning until dusk on Magazine Day, carriages would be halting before the entrances of the stores, while subscribers went in to purchase their favorite periodicals.

John Riley was then employed by the Bradstreet's financial reporting company and Martin Riley had a position as clerk in the Marion County courthouse. Both men were glad to see Jim and to spend their leisure hours with him. Even so, he was much alone, wandering, thinking. Probably during that period of waiting many residents saw and remarked upon the rather pale young man who drifted about the Circle or sat on a bench in the grass plot. He was slender, just under medium height, smooth-shaven now, with a wide mouth which seemed always to be tilting into a smile and China-blue eyes that had a far-off, reflective expression. His hair, once so blond, had darkened to brown and lay soft and smoothly-brushed above his high forehead. His clothes were of conservative cut, not expensive in ·quality, but meticulously clean and neat. Into the pocket of his coat was tucked a pair of gold-rimmed spectacles.

In the afternoon of October 16, Jim sauntered about before the New Park Theater, stealing sidelong glimpses at the bills nailed up in lobby and foyer. His name was on those bills—and he thought wryly of that long-ago time in Monrovia and the difficulties he had braved there. Since then he had made strides, but tonight was fateful. The city around him seemed vast, and he marveled at his temerity, his conceit, in believing that he could even temporarily focus its interest upon himself.

With twilight, a thin drizzle of rain fell. Jim sighed. "This cooks my goose," he thought. Surely no one would venture out into the rain to see and hear him.

He was standing near a lamppost, depressed and shivering. From the mists a figure emerged; it was the boy whose task was to turn on the gas and kindle the jets in the lamps; he had a short ladder over his shoulder and in his hand a wax, flame-tipped taper.

" 'Scuse me, sir." The boy propped his ladder against the post and, agile as a monkey, climbed up to touch the gas jet. Jumping down, he gestured toward the theater. "Goin' to have a show in there at eight o'clock. Some feller from Greenfield crackin' jokes."

"That so?" said Jim. "D'you know anything about him?"

"Well, the papers have been boostin' him and braggin' on him. A country yap, I guess."

"Ah?" said Jim.

"But he's a Hoosier, that ought to make him all right."

"It should, yes."

"And General Macauley is puttin' on the show. He's smart. People always take to his shows like ducks to water. They may take to this one."

"I hope they will," Jim muttered.

The New Park was opulent, bright, with all seats filled. Jim stepped out upon the stage and knew that, at least, he did not want for an audience. General Macauley introduced him, doing it smilingly, ingratiatingly, his arm linked with Jim's. Then the General retired—and Jim battled with an instant of stage fright.

But in his wallet was a little letter of encouragement from Elva May; in his buttonhole was a flower which his

181

sister Mary had sent, with best wishes for "peals of applause and encores ringing in your ears." Johnty was out there in the house somewhere, and Uncle Mart; a dozen friends had come from Greenfield. Suddenly Jim felt that there was no hostility in the atmosphere, only cordiality. These people were *all* his friends. And then he was calm, bowing, with that punctilious, courteous little movement from the waist which was habitual with him.

"Ladies and gentlemen," Jim said . . .

He soon knew that he had reached them; after a halfhour he had captivated them. He finished his program and they called him back; again and again he was encored. They would not let him go.

Later a group of men gathered outside the theater: George Harding and Berry Sulgrove, journalists and dramatic critics; Judge Martindale, owner of the *Indianapolis Journal;* the Reverend Mr. Myron Reed, pastor of the First Presbyterian Church.

"In my column tomorrow," said Harding, "I shall praise Riley to the skies. My opinion is that he's to have a national fame, and it will be a satisfaction to us to have attested our appreciation before everybody else does."

"Yes," said Sulgrove. "A couple of years and he'll be the most sought-after lecturer in America. James Whitcomb Riley is on the way to an enduring reputation."

Judge Martindale nodded. "Indiana has never been at a loss for writers. Charles Major, Edward Eggleston, Lew

"Ladies and gentlemen," he began.

Wallace, Ridpath—I could name you a hundred. But Riley—well, he seems *unique*."

"He is just that," said Mr. Reed. "I met him on Memorial Day last year. He recited his poem, *The Silent Victors*, at Crown Hill. I knew then that he would succeed. We have become good friends, Riley and I, a fact of which I'm very proud."

"If you are his friend, Reed," said Judge Martindale, "maybe you can persuade him to come to Indianapolis."

"To live?"

"Yes. I've been buying his verses quite a while now and running them in the *Journal*. More than once I've suggested that he join my staff. I want him badly. And for his own sake," said Judge Martindale, "he should be here. I feel that he belongs to us."

"He does," agreed Mr. Reed. "And I'll tell him so. This has been a fine evening, hasn't it?"

"One," said Sulgrove, "which Jim Riley and all of us will remember, I think."

Chapter Seventeen

THERE IS A certain disadvantage in living in the town where you were born and raised," wrote Myron Reed. "Whatever you may become, people grade you down to where you were. . . . If you have ever done anything ridiculous—and you have—it is remembered. Come West, young man, come to Indianapolis."

Jim pondered over that letter. Judge Martindale was offering a salary of twenty-five dollars a week; and the logic of Myron Reed was not to be denied. Greenfield was no more offending than any other town, but Jim sometimes felt that it had only tolerance for him and was too prone to hark back to the days of his shiftless boyhood. He was thirty years old now; if he meant ever to do great things—

Yet he hesitated. In scattering his poems to the four winds of the weeklies he was earning enough for his frugal needs. The Morgue and the Crow's Nest were snug "literary dens." And he knew his own frailties, how hard it was for him to knuckle down to routine, how occasionally he succumbed to laziness, the wish for remote horizons. If he could just loiter around an office, writing when the spirit moved, idling between times—that would be fine! A treadmill of duties was the thing he dreaded, having to produce copy as it was demanded, as if his poetry streamed from a spigot which could be turned on or off at will. Then, too, he had the notion that poetry was not a commodity, to be written on order, for money.

Nevertheless, in November, 1879, Jim was joining Judge Martindale's staff, assigned to a desk in the editorial rooms on the ground floor of the *Journal* building.

Myron Reed had warned that Jim must be dealt with leniently, a policy with which Judge Martindale was in accord, and so the newcomer was granted much freedom and told to make himself at home. He was to write nothing but poetry, and that only when he cared to.

"I knew Riley would come high," said Judge Martindale, "but I had to have him and would have paid any price to get him."

At first Jim spent little time at his desk. Instead, he strolled the streets, peering quizzically at passers-by, looking, listening, absorbing impressions. The city somewhat bewildered him and he was often lonely for the quiet seclusion he had left. He said in a letter to a Greenfield friend that there "are lots of features about it that are lovely, but the racket and rattle of it all is positively awful."

In the office he was so reserved and bashful that he could scarcely be drawn into conversation with the other reporters. The desk next his was occupied by Harry S. New, a stalwart and dashingly handsome young man who was detailed to writing police court items. While New briskly went at his daily stint, Jim would dawdle, sketching silly pictures or decorating a sheet of paper with intricately fancy borders.

"When do you write your stuff, Riley?" New would ask.

"Oh, I do that in my off-hours," Jim would answer, "at home. I can't think of rhymes here. I must have solitude."

Harry New was a sociable person and, having liked Jim at sight, he cultivated him. After the last edition had gone to press, he would take Jim and perhaps several others from the office to Pop June's restaurant where, over a plate of excellent food and a pot of coffee, Jim would slowly relax and begin to talk naturally and fluently. Despite the shyness, New considered him as fascinating a chap as he had ever known. His stories were enthralling, his humor contagious. Soon the two were devoted comrades.

The "home" which Jim had mentioned to Harry New was a draughty, dingy room upstairs in an old disused flat near the *Journal*. The faded, scaling walls once had been lined with posters advertising theatrical troupes. The furnishings consisted of a sagging cot, covered with dusty quilts, three chairs and a pine table. Jim named the place the Dead Rose and made no effort to renovate or improve it, except to put a terra cotta bust of Charles Dickens on a bracket above the table. He hung his clothes on nails which some former tenant had conveniently pounded into the door panels; he stacked his books in a corner, and then he was settled.

He could have had many callers, for the dwellers below stairs were all actors "at liberty," waiting for engagements or convivial bachelors who had no work and were not looking for it; but Jim shut himself away from them and wrote assiduously. Sometimes for twenty-four hours he would bend over his table, writing, revising, finishing a poem for the *Journal* or one to be submitted to a magazine. Then, stiff and cold to the marrow of his bones, he would stumble down the steps, dodge through the alley and eat a slab of apple pie or a cheese sandwich in some grimy little cafe.

Though consistently rebuffed by *Scribner's* and other first-rate periodicals, Jim was indomitable in his wish to make them conscious of him. To that end he began an assault upon the *New York Sun*. Charles A. Dana, the eminent editor there, was lukewarm. Riley's poetry lacked dignity, he said, and suggested that the Hoosier had better learn to spell and punctuate. Then, relenting, Mr. Dana said that Riley did seem to have the glimmerings of talent. Faint praise!—but Jim greedily snapped it up. To a ravenously hungry man even a crumb is nourishment. At long last Mr. Dana bought a poem from him—and then more.

During the winter Jim lectured in Indiana towns, hating the snow, the bad weather—and the trains. Such minor catastrophes as missing connections, getting on the wrong train or getting off the right one at the wrong station, losing his luggage or himself were to become the bane of his existence with the years.

Once, at Spencer, Indiana, in the hotel sitting-room, he saw Robert J. Burdette, the Baptist clergyman and former editor of the Burlington, Iowa, *Hawkeye,* who now was a humorous and immensely popular lecturer. The previous evening Burdette had spoken in Spencer on "The Rise and Fall of the Mustache," while Jim had been in Bloomington, reading verses.

After shaking hands, the two men compared notes as to their platform experiences. Riley said he had held the Bloomington janitor spellbound for an hour and a half; Burdette said his audience had been the club officials who engaged him and scarcely anyone else. In a few moments they were chuckling together over breakfast. Then Burdette went to Indianapolis with Jim.

This crossing of their paths was to have results. Burdette thought Riley effervescent, refreshing. He heard some of Jim's poems, a prose sketch or two. When he was at home in Burlington he wrote to the bigger lecture bureaus with which he himself was affiliated, recommending the Hoosier.

"I never heard him say a tiresome word or utter a tiresome sentence. I would walk through the mud or ride through the rain to hear him again. I would get out of bed to listen to him. If I have a friend on a lecture committee in the United States, I want to whisper in his ear that one of the best hits he can make will be to surprise his audiences with J. W. Riley . . . His humor is gentle; it is not caustic . . . Riley is good clean through."

Afterward, at least once every year, Robert Burdette visited Jim in Indianapolis where, with Myron Reed, they formed a rollicking trio.

When Jim had been seven months with the *Journal,* its ownership was transferred to John C. New. Mr. New was the father of Harry, the young police court reporter. A sterner drillmaster than Judge Martindale, he changed the editorial policies. He wanted witty articles from Jim Riley, and they must be ready on the dot each day.

This was a problem to Jim, and a nuisance. He solved it by keeping on file a supply of nondescript jottings, book reviews, skits, stories suffused with local color, oddments written in spare moments. With these he never was caught napping, but always had something to whip out at the call of the copy-boy. Quantity was the requirement, instead of

191

quality; he adjusted himself to the scheme. One thing he would *not* do, he said; that was to neglect his poetry for the drudgery of the office.

In three years he was to write more than three hundred poems, a tremendous output by any standard. Candidly sentimental, appealing to the emotions rather than the intellect, reflecting his bland optimism, his faith in God and in his fellowmen, these were to form the bulk of his work. Some would be sunny, some mournful. He wrote often of death; it had no terrors for him since a belief in the soul's immortality was the firmest of his convictions. "There are no dead," he maintained, and meant it.

Jim fell in love. It wasn't the first time; he had always enjoyed feminine society and had been casually smitten in the past. In Greenfield he had known Miss Louise Bottsford, a pretty young woman who was also a poet, of sorts; enough, anyway, for Jim to feel that their writing was a bond and to bring Miss Bottsford flitting into the Morgue, where she helped him with his verses and he composed lines to her goodness and her beauty. Though the Morgue may not have seemed just the setting for it, the little romance had flourished there a while, before Miss Bottsford bestowed her affections elsewhere.

Now Jim was again "hungering for woman's companionship," as he said; and the object of his new infatuation was again a poet—Ella Wheeler, soon to gain notability as Ella Wheeler Wilcox, a Wisconsin girl who

was as indefatigable in her own "literary den" as ever
Jim Riley was in his.

Miss Wheeler's debut had been at Madison, where one
of her compositions had been read at a reunion of the
Army of the Tennessee and had won the commendations
of General Sheridan, General Sherman, General Grant,
and the nation's press. Jim, in Indiana, had been following
her career, always with more interest. At last he addressed
her:

"For years, I have been wanting to find you that I might
tell you how much I like your writings—"

Her acknowledgment of his letter was tardy, but
gracious. She said she wasn't sure she had the gift of song.
"If I have, I am chosen of the gods, even as you are, and
we go with them—you and I—up into the mountain tops
and down into the deep valleys. I thank Heaven every
time I suffer and I bow my head with reverence every time
I am joyous, because I know what it all means. My thank-
fulness is unutterable."

To Jim this feeling of the Wisconsin poet's seemed
entirely comprehensible. He knew "what it all meant."
Here was a girl he could love and understand; "a God-
woman," Jim said to himself, "like Elizabeth Barrett,"
whom he, the American Browning, could court—and
marry! He must see her, must talk with her!

The chance came in June when he went with Myron
Reed for a northern hunting trip. Miss Wheeler was then
in Milwaukee, Jim called on her there. He never told

anyone of his impressions of that afternoon; but he wrote to Miss Wheeler from the hunting lodge, and on his way home he stopped over for a second time. Back in Indianapolis, he penned her a long letter and through the summer he wrote repeatedly, sending her drafts of his poems, addressing her as "Dear Filigree" and by other quaint and fanciful names, telling her of his work, his thoughts and ambitions.

Miss Wheeler's answers, never immediate, became more spaced by intervals of silence. Then she hinted delicately of the "waning strength" of her regard. Jim was distraught. Why the waning? What had he done? Miss Wheeler answered that she feared the marriage of two poets would not survive. The Brownings, Elizabeth and Robert, had been happy? Yes, but they were the exception. For the marriage of two American poets, Miss Wheeler was none too hopeful.

Thereafter, the correspondence lapsed—

Years later, Miss Wheeler spoke freely of the blighted love affair.

Mr. Riley, she said, had written a parody of one of her own poems, with the stanza:

> "He sat beside her in her home;
> He let her call him 'Jim.'
> She let him hold her hand in his,
> Which was great fun for him.
> Alas, alas, the woe that comes from calling
> fellows 'Jim!' "

194

"The wit and sparkle and beauty and pathos of his letters and my replies," said Miss Wheeler, "would, I know, have been delightful reading for the world today—had Mr. Riley and I remained correspondents only and never met. The meeting was precisely like the encounter of a canine and a feline. Mr. Riley certainly barked in a way which caused my feline back to rise, and instead of calling him 'Jim' I hissed in his face.

"I attired myself for his call in a new gown—one of the first really modish gowns I had ever owned. I remember it was black with little pipings of pale blue, quite in the fashion. My hair also was arranged in the fashion of the hour. The front was cut in a full fluffy 'bang' which everybody wore just then. I had at that time a radiant bloom; and I went to meet my caller, thinking my black and cerulean gown was very becoming. Not so Mr. Riley. He began at once to criticize me, announcing himself as bitterly disappointed in my 'frivolous appearance.' My dress and banged hair he thought most inappropriate for a 'genius,' and hearing that I had attended a lawn party that afternoon where there had been dancing, he expressed himself still more violently. Only idiots with their brains in their feet, he said, cared about dancing. I should be above such things.

"My own shock when I first saw Mr. Riley had been very great. He was very blond and very ugly. I was never attracted by blond men, even when handsome, and his whole personality was most disappointing to me. I did

195

not tell him so, but I did tell him that I considered him most impertinent . . ."

Of the second conversation, Miss Wheeler said: "He tried to be a bit conciliatory—and hoped we could be friends after all. But his next letter was so disagreeable that I wrote and asked him to return, at once, every letter I had ever written, as I did not want posterity to know I had wasted so much time on an impossible person."

Jim must have mused that love is an unpredictable thing, but he was reticent, saying nothing except (with a grin) that he would "die unmarried, unwept, and unsung." Perhaps the waning regard was not alone on Miss Wheeler's side. Jim had conjured in his mind an ideal which was the composite of all the sweet and beautiful women he had ever seen. It may be that no girl could have embodied it. The one he loved must always be an exquisite creature without reality—*"An Old Sweetheart of Mine."*

And Jim was poor, too. Perhaps he thought of that. A wife would have been an encumbrance, a responsibility. He had never assumed responsibilities; he may have been glad there was no necessity for it now. . . .

He was to see Ella Wheeler once more in his lifetime. That was eighteen years later; she was Mrs. Wilcox then, and famous though she was, Riley's eminence towered over hers. He stood in the corridor of a New York hotel as the smartly attired little lady stepped from the elevator.

She had not changed so much; he knew her. And she came forward, smiling.

"Mr. Riley!"

"Mrs. Wilcox." He bowed.

"I have some young people with me. Will you shake hands with them? They would be so pleased!"

"I'm sorry. I never do that sort of thing. It bores me."

"But, Mr. Riley—"

"No, Mrs. Wilcox."

Affronted, she looked at him. "You are a very selfish man," she said. "You do not deserve your success."

Jim shrugged, and turned away.

He was to meet another of his ideals, and this experience was gloriously satisfying. In January, 1882, he lectured in Boston, from the very rostrum in Tremont Temple where Dickens had spoken so many years before. It was a hallowed place to Jim. With his treatise, "Poetry and Character," and his poems he made a conquest of the city, his first important engagement beyond the borders of his native state. Boston warmed to him; John Boyle O'Reilly, the poet and editor, took him in charge and for a week wined and dined him.

But all this was as nothing when contrasted with his happiness at being invited to Craigie House, Longfellow's home.

"Come into my study," the great man said. He was

aging and infirm, but still a figure of nobility, with his white beard and crested white head. "It is more like freedom in here, Mr. Riley. We can talk and be content."

Jim was more than content; he was pink and tongue-tied. But Longfellow's cordiality was genuine, soon Jim had found his voice.

"I wrote you a letter once—"

"Yes, yes. I haven't forgotten."

"You told me you saw something in my work, a faculty which should be cultivated."

"And you have done so, Mr. Riley. You are going on with your poetry?"

"Oh, yes, constantly. That is my calling, to write. I lecture because I must earn money and because it brings me nearer to the people, so that I can truly know them. And to recite my poems is to circulate them more widely, and—" He paused—"to lighten the hearts of my listeners. I like to make men and women and children happy. I believe my platform appearances do that."

Longfellow discussed other American poets; he knew them every one, he said, and loved them, even the humblest.

"Will you read your *Old-Fashioned Roses* for me, Mr. Riley?"

"Indeed, I will." With alacrity Jim read the verses.

"Delightful!" Longfellow exclaimed. "Delightful!"

It was an accolade such as Jim had never dared to hope for!

198

Chapter Eighteen

ONCE JIM HAD counseled another poet, Captain Lee O. Harris, to drop his pen name so that he might more thoroughly enjoy the recompense of praise. Jim himself had been the recipient of like instruction from friends who watched his career. Certain tricks, these friends said, when Jim was writing the John C. Walker series, were beginning to be understood by the public and should be abandoned. Subterfuges would serve him no longer; he must depend upon merit to sustain him. An admirer in Illinois had begged him: "Shed your *nom de plume,* and shed it soon. Do you not see that this robs you of half your fame? Don't let your laurels go sailing round on eddying winds."

But Jim, though conscious of the folly of it, continued

to set his little snares for unsuspecting readers; and this, in 1882, gave rise to the Benjamin F. Johnson of Boone episode, perhaps the most notable of his masquerades. As a matter of fact, Jim thought of Benjamin F. Johnson so persistently and visualized the man so clearly that he never thereafter could quite dismiss the creation from his mind. Years later in a prose sketch, Jim described the old farmer of sixty-five with such detail as would indicate how real he had become to Jim's imagination—the wholesome, weathered countenance and cheerfully bright smile. "He wore a low-crowned, broad-brimmed felt hat on his broad, bronzed brow," recounted Jim, "and an old-styled frock-coat, but a clean white shirt and collar of one piece, with a string-tie and double bow beneath a long white beard."

The legend made its bow in the *Indianapolis Journal* on June 17, under the caption of "A Boone County Pastoral," with appropriate editorial comment:

"Benj. F. Johnson of Boone County, who considers the *Journal,* a 'verry valubul' newspaper, writes to inclose us an original poem, desiring that we kindly accept it for publication, as 'many neghbers and friends is asking him to have same struck off.'

"Mr. Johnson thoughtfully informs us that he is 'no edjucated man,' but that he has 'from childhood up till old enugh to vote, always wrote more or less poetry, as many of an album in the neghborhood can testify.' Again he says that he writes 'from the hart out'; and there is a touch of genuine pathos in the frank avowal, 'There is times when I write the tears rolls down my cheeks.'

"In all sincerity, Mr. Johnson, we are glad to publish the poem you send, and just as you have written it. That is its greatest charm. Its very defects compose its excellence. You need no better education than the one which emanates 'The Old Swimmin'-Hole.' It is real poetry, and all the more tender and lovable for the unquestionable evidence it bears of having been written 'from the hart out.' The only thing we find to criticize at all, relative to the poem, is your closing statement to the effect that 'it was wrote to go to the tune of "The Captain With His Whiskers!"' You should not have told us that, O Rare Ben Johnson!"

There followed the stanzas of the pastoral, beginning:

"Oh! the old swimmin'-hole! whare the crick so still and deep
  Looked like a baby-river that was laying half asleep,
  And the gurgle of the worter round the drift jest below
  Sounded like the laugh of something we onc't ust to know
  Before we could remember anything but the eyes
  Of the angels lookin' out as we left Paradise;
  But the merry days of youth is beyond our control,
  And it's hard to part ferever with the old swimmin'-hole." ...

The next week, on June 24, the Boone County contributor offered his *Thoughts Fer the Discuraged Farmer,* and the *Journal* was saying editorially: "It is a pleasure for us to note that the publication of the poem of 'The Old

Swimmin'-Hole' has proved almost as great a pleasure to
its author as to the hosts of delighted readers who have
written or called to personally indorse our high opinion
of its poetic value." Accompanying this was a letter, pur-
portedly from Mr. Johnson, and printed in full, even to
the postscript: "N. B.—The tune of this one is 'The Bold
Privateer.'"

As Jim had foreseen, Benjamin F. Johnson was an instant sensation in Indiana, and particularly in the region
of Boone County where the effort was immediately made
to find him. With the publication of *A Summer's Day* on
July first, excitement flourished; Boone County combed
its hills and dales: who and where was the elusive poet?
Then appeared *A Hymb of Faith,* and two weeks later,
Worter-melon Time:

"Old worter-melon time is a-comin' round again,
  And they ain't no man a-livin' any tickleder'n me,
  Fer the way I hanker after worter-melons is a sin—
  Which is the why and wharefore, as you can plainly see." . . .

Now the search for Johnson had been exhausted. He
was a myth, Hoosiers declared, a figment of someone's
fancy. But echoes reverberated from eastern and western
distances. A Harvard professor had read the five poems
and was eagerly awaiting more. In a Pacific coast university town, it was being claimed that Benjamin F. Johnson
was indeed an actual person. "Formerly he has written
under the pseudonym of 'James Whitcomb Riley.' Johnson
is real enough—and *Riley* is the myth!" One western

202

newspaper said that Johnson had the soul of a poet and the *Indianapolis Journal* had been guilty of gross offense in "contemptibly holding up to public scorn the simple old fellow's errors in grammar and spelling."

Meanwhile, on July 29, Johnson was again in print with *My Philosofy,* the concluding stanzas of which are:

> "The signs is bad when folks commence
> Afindin' fault with Providence.
> And balkin' 'cause the earth don't shake
> At ev'ry prancin' step they take.
> No man is great till he can see
> How less than little he would be
> Ef stripped to self, and stark and bare
> He hung his sign out anywhere.
>
> My doctern is to lay aside
> Contensions, and be satisfied.
> Jest do your best, and praise er blame
> That follers that, counts jest the same.
> I've allus noticed grate success
> Is mixed with troubles, more or less,
> And it's the man who does the best
> That gits more kicks than all the rest."

Of course, not everybody had been deceived. Jim's more discerning friends had guessed from the start the true identity of the Boone County rhymester. Myron Reed chuckled; and from his home in Pennsylvania, Robert Burdette wrote: "Glad to hear from you, glad to read Mr. Johnson's poems; glad to know who Mr. Johnson is." *My*

203

Philosofy had been revealing. "That's Jim Riley!" his friends exclaimed. "Couldn't be anyone else! Why, it's just like him!" But for people unacquainted with Jim there was no enlightenment; far and wide the farmer-poet was hailed as a literary discovery.

All through August Jim pursued this amusing bit of fooling. He was writing other verses, at the rate of two a day, but Benjamin Johnson was his chief interest. He knew he couldn't keep the endearing old fellow indefinitely before the public. No, sometime—and perhaps soon —the illusion must be dissolved. But for the present the Boone County contributor was very precious!

"I've got so," Jim said, "I believe in Johnson! I can *see* him. And I love him!"

Six more poems Johnson wrote. Then, on September 16, with *The Clover,* the twelfth and last of the series, came the disclosure.

"This author," confessed the *Journal,* "is Mr. James Whitcomb Riley . . . Those who have looked to the Saturday *Journal* for Benj. F. Johnson's quaint but truly poetic contributions will miss them from our columns, but they will be repaid with other literary work from Mr. Riley's muse."

Of the twelve poems, all stamped with Riley's distinctive facility for graceful rhythm, all in dialect, and all destined to survive, none is more typical an example or more often quoted than

Hoosier Poet

"When the Frost Is on the Punkin"

When the frost is on the punkin and the fodder's in the shock,
And you hear the kyouck and gobble of the struttin' turkey-
cock,
And the clackin' of the guineys, and the cluckin' of the hens,
And the rooster's hallylooyer as he tiptoes on the fence;
O it's then's the times a feller is a-feelin' at his best,
With the risin' sun to greet him from a night of peaceful rest,
As he leaves the house, bareheaded, and goes out to feed the
stock
When the frost is on the punkin and the fodder's in the shock.

They's something kindo' hearty-like about the atmosphere
When the heat of summer's over and the coolin' fall is here—
Of course, we miss the flowers, and the blossoms on the trees,
And the mumble of the hummin'-birds and buzzin' of the bees;
But the air's so appetizin', and the landscape through the haze
Of a crisp and sunny morning of the airly autumn days
Is a pictur' that no painter has the colorin' to mock—
When the frost is on the punkin and the fodder's in the shock.

The husky, rusty rustle of the tossels of the corn,
And the raspin' of the tangled leaves, as golden as the morn;
The stubble in the furries—kindo' lonesome-like, but still
A-preachin' sermons to us of the barns they growed to fill;
The strawstack in the medder, and the reaper in the shed;
The hosses in their stalls below—the clover overhead!—
O, it sets my heart a-clickin' like the tickin' of a clock,
When the frost is on the punkin and the fodder's in the
shock!"

So Jim regretfully said goodbye to Benjamin F. Johnson.

This time Jim's disguise had caused no resentment. Readers had been charmed by the poems and were asking the *Journal* for a publication in pamphlet form. Or, suggested someone, why not a book? . . . "Then we could have the Boone County bard and keep him, permanently!"

To publish a book? It was a thing Jim had dreamed of for years. He most emphatically wanted to do that. But how was he to tackle such a project? His ideas on practical matters were, and always would be, quite vague; all business dealings baffled him. There was, though, a man in the *Journal* office who was equal to any situation. This man was George C. Hitt, and Jim consulted him.

"Would the Johnson things make a book, George?"

"I think they would," Mr. Hitt said.

"Good!" Jim grinned. "I've got a name for it. *The Old Swimmin'-Hole and 'Leven More Poems.* Sounds like Ben, doesn't it?"

"And like Riley," said Mr. Hitt.

"Also like Hancock County, where I was born and raised. Everybody in Greenfield, everybody who knows the Brandywine will buy my book about the old swimmin'-hole. It will be Hoosier lore! . . . But we can't publish it in Indianapolis, for the city has no book-publishing concern. What can we do, George?"

After consideration, Mr. Hitt said that he would go to Cincinnati. "Robert Clarke and Company are leading publishers there. You clip the poems, Jim, and paste them on paper, one to a page. Get your manuscript in shape."

"Do you honestly suppose the Clarke company will accept it?"

"I honestly suppose so," said Mr. Hitt. "Yes, a few months more and you'll be the author of a book."

But in speaking with such certainty, Mr. Hitt had reckoned without his host—in this case a partnership of ultra-conservative publishers who fingered the crude manuscript with disdain. Dialect? It would not sell; moreover, it was uncouth. Robert Clarke and Company could not bring out under their seal a collection of trivial and inferior verse.

Mr. Hitt was crestfallen. How could he go back and tell Jim Riley of this rejection?

"Gentlemen, you are letting a golden opportunity slip by."

The gentlemen shook their heads.

"Mr. Riley is no hack writer. He will be a phenomenal success."

Individually and as a group the publishers murmured their dissent.

"Then," said Mr. Hitt, "will you print the book at my expense? I'll put up the money. And I know I can sell the books!"

Yes, this the company would do. One thousand copies would be printed, Mr. Hitt would bear the expense and his name would be on the title page, as publisher.

Through the long hot summer of 1883 Jim looked forward to seeing his book, scarcely believing that some irony of circumstance would not intervene. He had to go to Cincinnati to read the proof. The galleys in his hand brought him a queer feeling. "It's so!" he thought. "I'm really to publish a book!"

He was working very hard, sweltering by night over his table in the filthy, badly ventilated Dead Rose which was never swept, dusted or aired. But he did not complain. On the contrary he'd never been more buoyant. That wall of prejudice against which he had hammered, the eastern magazines, evidenced a weakening. He had submitted six poems to *Life;* all were bought and now he had at last crashed through, into the august sanctum of the *Century,* whose editor had remarked, when accepting *In Swimming-Time:* "I must say that there is nobody at present writing who seems, to me, to get so much of genuine human nature into a short space, as you have." And, as usual, the stream of Riley verse was flowing in the *Journal* and out to the Hoosier country weeklies, and thence to other newspapers in other localities.

The Old Swimmin'-Hole and 'Leven More Poems was a small volume ("about the size of a pocket Testament," thought Jim, "or of Frances Quarles' *Divine Emblems,* which I used to have under my pillow in the attic trundle-bed") but it was well. bound in imitation vellum. The printing was good, and Jim had written an attractive little preface for the context. Jim gave away one hundred and three copies; the rest Mr. Hitt sold at a retail price of fifty cents.

What most elated Jim was that the edition sold so quickly—and at a profit of $166.40!

Author and publisher argued over the distribution of the profit. Each insisted that the other must have it all. Finally they compromised and shared it.

Then Mr. Hitt contracted with Merrill, Meigs and Company of Indianapolis for a second edition, a facsimile of the first, except for a red border around the pages.

"You're to have the royalties, Jim—and there'll be some, never fear, worth having! As for me, I'm retiring from the publishing business, forever."

209

*H*E NUMBERED HIS Indianapolis friends literally by the thousands and they were amazingly assorted, from Benjamin Harrison, the most profound lawyer at the Marion County bar, to the ragamuffin bootblack who daily scampered up the steps to the Dead Rose to shine the poet's shoes—just for the fun of a minute's bantering with him. To these people and to Greenfield and all of Indiana, he was Jim and always would be, *"our* Jim." But to the world he was now Riley, the author. With the circulation of his book, letters came to him from John Hay, Robert Underwood Johnson, Mark Twain, Joel Chandler Harris and many other American writers, addressing him as one who had been graduated from apprenticeship and initiated into the literary brotherhood. Riley, said Myron Reed, had arrived.

There was demand, too, for his lectures. Robert Burdette had recommended to the Redpath Lyceum Bureau that he be listed with its star performers. The Hoosier Poet was top-notch. "If the house that greets Riley is half so large as his lecture is twice as good," Burdette said, "people's feet will stick out the dormer windows. After hearing him you will want him to come back again and again." And Josh Billings, the Yankee humorist, added his endorsement, characteristically:

"Deer Publik: I take extreem delite in introdusing 2 yure imediate notis my yung and handsum frend, Mr. James Whit Kum Riley, who iz a phunny man of purest ray sereen. He iz the only man i kno that plays his own hand, or, in wurds less profeshonal, the only man that gives his own produxions, and not other folks'. He iz phunnier than tung kan tell.

Yures without a struggle,
JOSH BILLINGS."

But even without such sponsorship, Riley would have had more engagements than he could ever have filled. As a recitationist of the kind then so popular, he had no peer.

The proprietors of the *Journal* were willing for him to spend whatever time was necessary to his lecture tours. Indeed, his connection with the Indianapolis newspaper during the middle '80's would be hard to define. He had a desk in the office but was almost never there. Yet he wrote regularly and furnished ample material. This, and the pride of having him as a fixture on the staff, apparently was all the *Journal* asked.

So, in the winter of 1883 and for many seasons thereafter, Riley was on the road with his program of entertainment which he called "Eccentricities of Western Humor." He gave both poetry and prose, as Josh Billings had said, "his own produxions," and nothing else. He went to most of the cities and small towns from Kansas to Maine, and back again. Each season his orbit expanded; and though traveling by train was never a pleasure to a man of his temperament—"hurry, worry, bother, bluster, anxiety, and hunger for companionship; strangers to the right of me, strangers to the left of me, the spiteful and convulsive jerking of the car"—he felt that the advantages outweighed the disadvantages. It was, perhaps, just one of the penalties exacted by a growing fame.

Often his path crossed that of some other celebrity, as in New York, when he met Matthew Arnold, the great English poet and critic, and rode with him to Boston. Riley had a naïve curiosity about Arnold, drawing him into conversation and later describing him to Myron Reed as "a gaunt raw-boned Britisher, with mutton-chop whiskers and a cowcatcher nose . . . as cold and inexpressive as an iceberg." Yet Riley, who liked everyone, felt an affection for Arnold and did not resent his somewhat caustic remarks upon America and Americans.

What Arnold may have thought about the Hoosier Poet has never been divulged.

Hoosier Poet

The summer months of 1885 Riley divided between vacationing at Greenfield and at Delphi, Indiana, a town which always welcomed him and where he had many beloved cronies. Along the banks of Deer Creek he fished a bit, but mostly he wrote, soothed by the yellow sunshine, refreshed by grass and flowers and trees. He was getting together the copy for a second book, which was to be titled *The Boss Girl*. There had been a new edition of *The Old Swimmin'-Hole* and he was mailing out complimentary volumes to authors "in domestic and foreign lands," even sending one to Robert Browning in London, with the wish that something of value might be found in it.

In the autumn of that year, at his father's house in Greenfield, Riley wrote what was to be his most widely read poem—and perhaps the best-loved poem ever written by anyone, anywhere, for children, about children, and in their language: *Little Orphant Annie*. That 1885 version was not its final one: it would be altered and perfected before the "little orphant's" adoption as an American classic. Temporarily Riley was calling the piece *The Elf Child* and its heroine "Allie"; but the substance of the poem was there, a reminiscence, whole and intact, of a memory indelibly marked, never fading: "Where—is—Mary—Alice—Smith?"

The Boss Girl was published in November, 1885, in paper covers adorned by a rather florid and fanciful picture which Riley had designed, with the assistance of

213

young Booth Tarkington, a schoolboy of sixteen then, a native of Indianapolis and one who would win immeasurable honor for himself, his city, and his state in the years ahead. Riley had sketched an ink bottle mounted like a cannon and discharging an explosion of black lines which formed the letters in the list of story titles. To this Booth Tarkington added the drawing of an imp leaning down out of clouds, to touch off the cannon with the quill pen in his hand.

The first edition of *The Boss Girl* sold readily, yet Riley was never quite satisfied with it. He hadn't had sufficient time to work over the proofs, and there were entire paragraphs which he would have stricken out, had he not been so rushed. The book was therefore a disappointment, for the most part and did nothing to further his reputation. The consensus of opinion among critics was that his domain was not prose but poetry, and he would do well to confine himself to that.

In February, 1886, Indianapolis saw the opening performance of what was to be a notable combination of lecturers. James Whitcomb Riley had allied himself with Bill (Edgar W.) Nye to launch a lengthy tour. For this showing in Riley's home city, Eugene Field had come down from Chicago, where he conducted his inimitable column, *Sharps and Flats,* on the staff of the *Daily News.*

As was expected, they played to an enormous house— "packed," said Robert Burdette, who was a spectator, "until people began to fall out of the windows." Of the three "funny men" on the platform, Nye was the most non-sensical buffoon, Field the maddest and much the clever-est, Riley the most convinced of his own talent. But that night all were at their comical best; the audience roared with laughter until the curtain rang down.

Field went with them a little way; then, wishing them good hunting and Godspeed, he returned to Chicago; and Riley and Nye set out on a journey which was to stretch for thousands of miles, an intricate web, over the country.

Riley wrote to Indianapolis friends that they were on the road constantly and attendance wasn't always so large that people fell out of the windows. But with the weeks they gained in patronage. Riley modestly attributed this growing popularity to Nye's drollery. Nye, he said, was superb; with such a teammate the trials of the tour were lessened—"I am almost content with what seems my prin-cipal mission here on earth, i. e., to spread over and run all around it like a ringworm."

As they went they were compiling something which they called *Nye and Riley's Railway Guide,* a hodgepodge of skits and jingles, mellow and farcical, which was to be published later with varying titles.

Like Riley, Bill Nye had the background of a writer. It was as a contributor to the Laramie, Wyoming, *Boom-erang* that he had caught the eye of Eugene Field, who was at that time editing a Denver newspaper. Field had known at once that the stalwart, bearded rancher stalking

215

into his Denver office with "copy," had possibilities as a professional entertainer.

"I discovered Nye," Eugene Field was wont to say. "The only nugget I ever panned out there in the gold rush. I dusted him off, rubbed up his rough edges—and now look at him!"

Nye was, in fact, a man of diverse experiences. Born in Maine, educated in Wisconsin, he had spent years of his adult life in the west, practicing law, teaching school, dabbling in politics, until his discovery as a punster and merry-andrew put him upon the lecture platform.

To Riley's consternation, Bill Nye was ill in the autumn, ordered by his physician to halt and go back to his home in New York. Riley must fare on alone.

The change in plans was more serious than Riley cared to admit. He had relied on Nye to see to all practical matters. Even the simple transaction of buying a railroad ticket was a mystery to Riley; once in the cars, he usually misplaced his ticket and, oftener than not, had forgotten to cash the check with which to buy another. In strange cities he was afraid to venture out into the streets, but would take a cab to the hotel (any hotel which the cab-driver suggested) and there sit for hours in the drab lobby behind the potted palms and rubber plants, until someone came to lead him to the theater or hall where he was slated for an engagement.

Trolleys he abhorred because, he said, he never knew at which end to get on or off them. When leaving a town

216

he would go very early to the station, would wait, his gaze glued to the track, his ear tuned for preliminary bells—and then miss the train. This had happened to him even in Indianapolis. He was hoodooed, he said; the proverbial scapegoat, the man in his poem:

> " 'Ll where in the world my eyes has bin—
> Ef I hain't missed that train ag'in!
> Chuff! and whistle! and toot! and ring
> But blast and blister the dasted train!—
> How it does it I can't explain!
> Git here thirty-five minutes before
> The durn thing's due—and, drat the thing!
> It'll manage to git past—shore!
>
> "The more I travel around, the more
> I got no sense!—To stand right here
> And let it beat me! 'Ll ding my melts!
> I got no gumption, ner nothin' else!
> Ticket Agent's a dad-burned bore!
> Sell you a ticket's all they keer!—
> Ticket agents ort to all be
> Prosecuted—and that's jest what!—
> How'd I know which train's fer me?
> And how'd I know which train was not? . . ."

How infinitely relieved, the "Train-Misser" must have been when, in the spring of 1887, Bill Nye rejoined him!

On a morning in November, 1887, Riley received an important invitation. It was from the Executive Committee of the International Copyright League, asking him to participate in the Authors' Readings which would be held in Chickering Hall, New York, on the 28th and 29th of that very month.

". . . Lowell will preside and Curtis, Clemens, Cable, Howells, Stockton, Warner, Eggleston and Page will read from their own works. It will be a great occasion and worth your while to come."

He was astounded—and happy. He had been yearning to go to New York. He knew what the League was and that it had been meeting annually for a decade. Never before had he been invited. Perhaps the fact that now the *Century* was publishing his poems, that *The Old Man and Jim* and others of his compositions had excited praise in the magazines, accounted for the Executive Committee's benevolent attitude. Anyway, it was an auspicious omen, a recognition which, as he told Myron Reed, "the little bench-leg poet" must not refuse. He had been busily preparing for a new book, *Afterwhiles,* which the Bowen-Merrill Company of Indianapolis would publish. But— to be introduced in New York by James Russell Lowell! "Only think of it!" he exclaimed, and forthwith resolved to invade the east, challenge what he had felt to be its hostility—and read dialect!

On the first day of the Authors' Readings the pavements and stairs outside Chickering Hall were densely thronged and carriages were having to stop at the corner a block

218

away where policemen steered the traffic. Inside, the audience exceeded seating capacity; people were wedged several rows deep around the walls of the auditorium, craning their necks to glimpse the illustrious persons occupying the chairs on the stage. There was an alert rustling as James Russell Lowell stepped forward; he was a venerable figure, a man sagacious, polished, experienced in diplomatic affairs as well as in literature, honored in his own country and abroad. It was fitting that Lowell should preside at this event; he was vigorously applauded, then the audience hushed.

On the platform, as the program opened, Riley strove to conceal his perturbation. He was immaculately groomed, well and tastefully dressed, he did not doubt his own powers, he had confidence in his poetry. It was sincere, he thought; it was real and had vitality and needed no explanation or apology. Yet he knew that as never before he faced now an audience of intellectuals, and whether or not he could gain their approval remained to be seen. This was a testing, as once General Macauley's benefit had been; but then he had been among friendly Hoosier folk. Here he was regarded more or less as an interloper. He thought that he could see in the front row interrogating countenances, as if one patron were nudging his neighbor and inquiring: "Who is that? The slender little man with the smile and the eyeglasses? James Whitcomb Riley? But who is *he?*"

219

"I'll have to show them," he thought.

His place on the program was just after that of George W. Cable who had been dramatic and effective. When Lowell had finished with a short introduction and had bowed, Riley got slowly up and approached the footlights. He was apprehensive, his hands rather moist. But, as had so often occurred, he lost all fear the minute he began to speak. He became the actor, poised and sure of himself. He read *When the Frost Is on the Punkin,* and he was not Mr. Riley at all but Benjamin F. Johnson of Boone County, Indiana, that lovable old farmer who wrote his poems "from the hart out."

He knew even before he was encored that he had pleased and surprised the audience. He could see and hear and feel the warmth of their response. And, back at his hotel, he had concrete evidence of it, in the newspaper reports. "He sailed in," one said, "as though he had been born to the stage and gave a performance that the most illustrious comedian might envy." He must be acknowledged "the position in American literature which his genius and versatility deserve." "As excellent a piece of mimicry as Chickering Hall ever saw, capping the climax of the afternoon's enjoyment," declared the *Herald;* and the *New York World* called him "the stranger and the success of the occasion." . . . "The fun of the other authors shriveled up into bitter patches of melancholy in the bright light of Riley's humor."

But his triumph was not to end there. On the second

day, at the close of the program, James Russell Lowell made a totally unlooked-for announcement.

"Ladies and gentlemen," he said, "I want to thank you for your kind attention without which these readings could not have been a success. I also desire to thank Mr. James Whitcomb Riley, who has so generously consented to favor us again today with one of his delightful selections. I confess with no little chagrin and sense of my own loss, that when yesterday afternoon I presented him to a similar assemblage, I was almost a stranger to his poems. Since then I have been reading one of his books, and in it I have discovered so much of high worth and tender quality that I deeply regret that I had not long before been acquainted with his work. I have been so impressed with the tenderness and beauty of the poems that I read that I almost hope he will give one of them now. But whether it be one I have read or something else, I am sure it will be something good. Today, in presenting him, I can say to you of my own knowledge that you are to have the pleasure of listening to the voice of a true poet."

The demonstration which followed was overwhelming. Riley rose, advanced to the rostrum. The poem he recited was *Nothin' To Say,* one which had been published previously in the *Century,* the story of a father's emotion when told that his motherless daughter is going to be married. He could not have chosen more wisely, for *Nothin' To Say* had an appealing pathos and, as Riley gave it, a strong and moving simplicity of sentiment. After the last word

221

been before: it was music drawn from "the homely chords of Hoosierdom with the zeal of an artist and the love of a patriot." Prior to publication, thousands of the first edition were sold and subsequent editions were planned.

Riley was living then in the Indianapolis home of his sister Elva May who had married Mr. Henry Eitel, a widower with one charming little daughter, Harriet. In this environment he was singularly happy. After drifting so long from one furnished room to another no more cheerful, he was a member of a family circle, surrounded by affection and pleased with the experience. He had always been devoted to Elva May; he owed her husband a debt of gratitude for the assistance which Mr. Eitel, a competent business man, was rendering in the handling of the poet's affairs.

Riley himself had no understanding whatever of business. "He knew as much about it," said a friend, "as an Australian kangaroo knows about *The Iliad.*" His poems had been printed in the Indianapolis papers and in other journals and periodicals over the nation; enormous quantities of them were stored away in musty trunks. Nothing had ever been destroyed. Now that he was established and publishers were begging for manuscripts, he must bring some system from the chaos. With the help of Elva May and of a secretary, Mr. Eitel attacked the monumental task of accumulating and sorting the work of many years, a thing Riley never could have done, even had he wished to.

Hoosier Poet

Perhaps it would have been well if he had rested longer with the Eitels; but he was being besought on every side to lecture and, despite his plaints as to the vexations, he felt the lure of the open road. So, in February, 1888, he and Bill Nye were together again, sallying forth on a tour of the Middle West, regaling the Chicago Press Club and then going on to nearby cities and towns. As a South Bend wag put it, all the corn belt that spring shook with glee at their witticisms:

> "Nye and Riley, Riley and Nye:
> Grin and chuckle, sob and sigh!
> Never had such fun by half,
> Knew not whether to cry or laugh.
> Jest and joke and preach and sing,
> They can do most anything—
> Make you laugh or make you cry—
> Dear old Riley! Rare Bill Nye!"

In April Riley made his second visit to Chickering Hall and remained in New York for several days, becoming a familiar figure on Broadway. Ever a marvel of neatness in dress and personal habits, he strolled down the avenues of the metropolis, enveloped in his fine, fur-trimmed overcoat, his hat at a gallant angle, his blue eyes alight with merriment behind the gleaming spectacles. Rumor had it that the Hoosier poet was contemplating the writing of a series of political articles. Nothing could have been more absurd. Politics was quite beyond the realm of his

dead now, but his advice was not forgotten and never more would any grammarian have the chance to designate flaws in James Whitcomb Riley's diction.

In the spring of 1889 Riley and Nye were bound for the mountain regions and the Pacific slope, with every prospect of a good season; but then in April Nye was recalled by illness in his family; and Riley, unwilling to travel without him, returned to Indianapolis.

Somehow, in a manner difficult to define, this cancellation of their elaborate tour seemed to meet with approbation in many quarters. Perhaps they had been too prominently in the news for too long a period and were due for a reversal, a mild chiding from a public notoriously fickle. At any rate, newspapers in several cities commented. "It is fortunate," said the *Rochester Chronicle*. "Certainly the reputation of neither has been enhanced and the literary work which they have attempted to do in their travels, writing at hotels or on the cars, has been of a character decidedly inferior." The talented pair had been frittering away their time and strength, said the *Pittsburgh Dispatch*. "With a man of genius like Riley it is not necessary that he should make a circus of himself . . . his work is universally admired, and there is a keen demand for more of his delicious lyrics. They are not forthcoming. Perhaps he will abandon the circus business and resume the pursuit of the Muse. . . ."

Such editorials held a tone of subtle warning which Riley and Nye scoffed at and ignored.

228

Hoosier Poet

There was an organization in Indiana known as the Western Association of Writers, founded in 1886 and convening every summer at Winona. Most of the writers were amateurs, striving for recognition, though the roster also boasted of some "big names." From its start, Riley had been considerate of the infant organization and had served as a director and vice-president, had gone to its meetings and donated verses for its yearbooks. Its ideals he was wholly in sympathy with: to promote a literary fraternity in the midlands, to impart the spirit of fellowship among young writers, to encourage their groping beginnings. At the reunion of this group in July of 1888, he had read *Orphant Annie* and *The Old Man and Jim*, with its recurrent refrain of wistful leave-taking:

> " 'Well: goodbye, Jim
> Take keer of yourse'f!' "

He was, indeed, the darling of the W. A. W.; and nothing could have been more natural than that he should have been specifically thanked for his cooperation. This the association proceeded to do, with a gala dinner at the Denison Hotel in Indianapolis in October, 1888. The orations were many, all lauding the poet. Letters were read from Mark Twain, George William Curtis, from James Boyle O'Reilly of Boston and Benjamin Harrison, recently nominated as a candidate for the Presidency. It was the distinct understanding of the diners that, should Har-

agonies of self-reproach and uncertainty. What would the homefolks think of him? How would they react to his disgrace?

He was soon to learn. The Indianapolis Literary Club of leading jurists, clergymen, physicians and philanthropists, stated that it would entertain Mr. Riley at a reception "in appreciation of his achievements."

The reception was magnificent, and every masterly speech emphasized Indiana's abiding trust in her poetic son. At the close of an emotion-charged evening, Jim was prevailed upon to recite two selections while his hearers smiled and wept.

It was a Hoosier rally of astonishing proportions.

"Whitcomb Riley," said the *Chicago Mail,* "remains king on his native heath. . . . In this age a poet is not without honor in his own corner of the world!"

Chapter Twenty-one

ROBISON 41

AS IN THE case of the *Leonainie* trouble, the rumblings of this tempest shortly subsided and expired. Following the example of Indianapolis, other communities expressed their loyalty; Riley was the guest of the Blue Grass Club in Louisville, of the Glenarm Club in Denver. Meredith Nicholson, Hamlin Garland and Rudyard Kipling, three men of letters who were also stanch friends, cautioned him against the perils of intensive lecturing—and he heeded them. From now on he would write the greater part of the time, he said, and consent to platform engagements only occasionally.

Orders for poems were pouring in upon him; he could fill but a few, for he was assembling material for a new book, *Rhymes of Childhood,* delving into his files for precious fragments he had preserved there. These verses were pictures drawn from his own youth, of a child's joys and sorrows, intended for other boys and girls, destined to delight them and their like for generations. It was to be his best-loved book, just as childhood seemed to him the most vital phase of life. Perhaps though he was a man in years and stature, his emotions had never matured as a man's; at heart he was still the little Jim Riley, fascinated by the weaving commerce of the National Pike, playing clown in the hayloft, exploring the orchard and the Brandywine, knowing every villager and the hired men in the fields, the colts in the pastures and the goblins with green glass eyes that dwelt in the upstairs rafter-room and capered and postured on the back fence.

The fact was that youth had been the mainspring of his talent and now his activity consisted chiefly of revamping and improving poems written earlier. Most of his enduring verse was produced before his fortieth birthday; he had saved it, everything; now, when inspiration was so slow, so infrequent, he could release these poems as if they were quite fresh and new.

He was taking a lively interest in the composition of his books. With Mr. Eitel to supervise, he learned to be thrifty, to set a price upon his pen; in 1890 he began to be financially independent beyond his most sanguine hopes. The books were swiftly materializing, selling in such number as to bring him handsome royalties.

His residence was no longer with the Eitels. He would

always be a favorite guest there, adored and petted by Elva May's step-daughter and by her own daughter and her son. But when his sister's family had grown to five, Riley feared he was imposing on them. He said that he must not wear out his welcome. He rented a room at the Denison Hotel.

His father visited him there. John Riley was then in Albuquerque, New Mexico. Since John's departure, Mr. Reuben Riley had not often come to Indianapolis. He was old now and, as he said, "set in his ways."

"Father," the poet said, "I'm going to buy you a new outfit, from hat to shoes."

"Why? What's the matter with these things I've got on?" Mr. Riley demanded, with asperity. "Oh, I know. They'll do very well for a country lawyer—but not for the daddy of such a prominent man, eh?"

"Don't you remember the suit you made for me? You dressed me up and took me to the court house and exhibited me."

"And now it's your turn to exhibit. All right, Jim, you buy the rig. I'll put it on."

In the new clothes he walked with his son about the city.

"Everybody speaks to you, Jim. These folks all seem to love you. Why is that?"

"Maybe because of my affection for them. I write about them and they like it."

"I wish your mother could know!"

"She does," said Jim stoutly.

Mr. Riley mused. "I can't see why your rhymes should be worth so much money. What are they? Dialect! No, sir, I can't understand how you've got where you are! And I still think you should have been a lawyer, Jim. You'd have made a good lawyer!"

The Denison was a well-appointed, first-rate hotel. But Riley felt that there he was "living on the wing." As the years passed, he yearned to have a permanent home, an anchorage.

On a summer evening in 1893 he went to call upon his friend, Major Charles L. Holstein in Lockerbie Street. Riley had frequently dined with the Holsteins, a family consisting of the Major, his wife, and Mrs. Holstein's parents, Mr. and Mrs. Nickum. His acquaintance with Lockerbie Street was of even longer standing.

Once, in 1880, as he roved across town, he had stumbled upon the quiet little thoroughfare, two irregular squares in length, the houses shrubbery encircled, with flower beds above the sidewalks and maples and sycamores in majestic borders. Intrigued with that first sight, he had written a poem about it, which was printed in the *Indianapolis Journal,* and then in *Afterwhiles* and in *Old-Fashioned Roses:*

"Such a dear little street it is, nestled away
  From the noise of the city and heat of the day,

Hoosier Poet

In cool shady coverts of whispering trees,
With their leaves lifted up to shake hands with the breeze
That in all its wide wanderings never may meet
With a resting-place fairer than Lockerbie street!

There is such a relief, from the clangor and din
Of the heart of the town, to go loitering in
Through the dim, narrow walks, with the sheltering shade
Of the trees waving over the long promenade,
And littering lightly the ways of your feet
With the gold of the sunshine of Lockerbie street. . . .

O, my Lockerbie street! You are fair to be seen—
Be it noon of the day, or the rare and serene
Afternoon of the night—you are one to my heart,
And I love you above all the phrases of art,
For no language could frame, and no lips could repeat
My rhyme-haunted raptures o'er Lockerbie street."

The publication of this eulogy had surprised and pleased the householders in Lockerbie Street, and next morning they had dispatched big bouquets of their choicest garden flowers to the *Journal* office to bedeck the poet's table.

Tonight, walking along, seeing the children tumbling on the lawns or chasing after fireflies, the older folk seated on vine-hung verandas, hearing the "tinkle and beat" of a piano from an open casement, a snatch of song, the murmur of voices in conversation, Riley thought that to a bachelor like himself, Lockerbie Street signified all those

237

and black, with gold-leaf cornices. Chairs and sofas were ornate, overstuffed and tasselled, the upholstering of figured damask. An oval table centered the flowered carpet and supported a tall, silk-shaded lamp. At one end of the room a mirror stretched from floor to ceiling, lighted by a glass-globed gas fixture that matched the crystal chandelier. At the other end was a white marble fireplace.

Across the hall from the drawing-room, the library had bookshelves, a plush sofa, a velvet-seated cathedral chair an enormous cushioned easy chair (reserved, after Riley's coming, just for him), hassocks, a rattan smoking-stand, and a mantelled fireplace surmounted by candlesticks, vases, a bronze clock against an oblong, banded and decorated mirror.

Perhaps the finest room in the house was the dining-room, spacious and hospitable, the furniture heavy and elaborately carved and knobbed after the manner of nineteenth century fashion. The round table with its intricate four-branched base might have been a collector's item; the sideboard was a towering walnut structure, ornamented with shelves, topped with a splendid carving of plumed birds and an epergne of fruit. Here again the walls were panelled, the windows deep and heavily cased in glossy woodwork, with a pendulum clock set between them.

The "nook" which Major Holstein found for Riley was an airy chamber on the second floor, luxuriously carpeted, with a massive bed, Morris chairs, a rounded fireplace of

Here he received his young admirers.

mottled black marble. By installing a desk, shelves for his books, his pictures, the mask of Keats, the terra cotta of Dickens and other prized belongings, the poet made it his own.

When Riley went to Lockerbie Street—or Lockerbie Land, as he liked to say—it was, indeed, to stay. Of course he would be absent from it now and then, but briefly: he always hurried back, convinced that only here could he have the refuge so precious to him. To Lockerbie Street would come, soon or late, all the great and the near-great of the American literary scene, and other, simpler pilgrims too numerous to count, old and young, adults and children, each hoping for a glimpse of the Hoosier Poet.

His devotion to the city of Indianapolis was just as intense. He loved it. When some unavoidable errand or a passing restlessness took him away, he suffered from homesickness. Except in Indianapolis, he never could be himself, he said. Indianapolis was "high Heaven's sole and only 'understudy.' "

Chapter Twenty-two

IN 1891 RILEY sailed for Europe and there he wandered from one historical spot to the next, meditating
upon the strangeness of everything, the babel of
tongues unintelligible to him, the inclement weather,
evincing no liking for any of it. Except in those places
where poets had lived and written, he was apathetic. He
went to Dumfries, Scotland, and looked at the house in
which Robert Burns had died so prematurely, and could
have wept, he said, to see the "For Rent" placard above
the lintel and to think of the hardships which the Scottish
singer of immortal ballads had known, his poverty and
want. In London, Riley renewed his acquaintance with
Ellen Terry and Henry Irving and, as Irving's guest, attended the theater. Then he made his homeward voyage.

244

Europe was not for him; its traditions could not stir him. His own past, though, was ever vivid to him. He revelled in it, conjuring up his childhood. In writing of that he retained the youthful viewpoint, and added to it his skill as a versifier, his unerring sense of rhythm and rapid-moving, jingling sound. His poems for and about childhood were his best and most natural.

He hadn't forgotten his long-ago resolution to reclaim the Greenfield homestead. "Sometime," he had said, "it will be mine again." In the spring of 1893 he purchased it; and that summer, with his sisters and Mrs. Eitel's children, he spent several weeks of serenity there. The furnishings, left by the former owner, were scant; the visit was a sort of camping out; but Riley was rested by it. Here he could recapture the joys and sorrows he had known as a boy, could think of his mother. His one regret was that his father could not also occupy the house. Mr. Reuben Riley had died only a little while before—and very proud, in that last period of earthly existence, very pleased at Jim's accomplishments!

The years were kind to James Whitcomb Riley.

He must often have thought, as he aged so gracefully, so free from the cares and disillusionments which burden most men, how different was his own treatment at the hands of fate from that of the poor creature he had described in his poem, *Fame*. Writing those lines, struggling, embittered by defeat, he had been unable to visualize any surcease, any reward. He would perish, he thought; and only then, when he was cold and still, would fame come to him. Such, surely was the destiny of poets!

Yet this poet who was himself had miraculously survived—and his cup held full measure, brimmed over. Fame was his!

Having it, he was rather awed, rather doubtful. He had been granted so much, more than he had ever anticipated, more than he could have imagined. Should it all be his, the little bench-leg poet's?

There was, perhaps, no logical explanation for his extraordinary success. He was not a scholar, never a man who studied deeply or with discrimination. Many branches of learning he had not touched upon; into most subjects he had investigated only superficially. But he was gentle, honorable, innately modest; he loved his fellowmen and had been watchful of them, alert to their ways and whimsicalities, believing in them and the God they worshipped—and he had dreamed a lot. This and his insatiable ambition, his incessant effort, may account for him. He had been certain of himself, positive that he had a mission, and a worthy one, to write about the people, and for them, and thus to make them happy. By sheer persistence, force of will, he had dominated. Now the world accepted him at his own evaluation.

All the things he had desired came to him. Like a parade of conquering soldiers his books marched from the press—*The Flying Islands of the Night, Green Fields and*

Hoosier Poet

Running Brooks, Poems Here at Home, Armazindy, A Child-World, Rubaiyat of Doc Sifers, Love-Lyrics, Home-Folks, Farm-Rhymes, and dozens of other editions compiled from the contents of these volumes. With the books came wealth. When now he lectured, it was according to his own terms, at his convenience. With every book, every public performance, his popularity increased. T. C. Steele painted him; he sat to John Singer Sargent for as fine a portrait as any ever executed by that eminent Anglo-American artist. By the turn of the century no man in the United States was more widely-known or generally beloved than James Whitcomb Riley, none more likely to become a national legend.

He was preparing his *Book of Joyous Children* then, with its dedication to Joel Chandler Harris, whose friendship he so prized. In the spring of 1900 he had visited the Harrises in Georgia, two weeks which were, he said, "a bewilderingly gorgeous dream." "Uncle Remus" was a fictional character which delighted Riley. As for the animals in Harris' stories, they were all quite real to him, "Bre'r Rabbit," "Sis 'Possum," "Bre'r 'Coon"—lapsing into Negro dialect, Riley would discuss them with Harris, their creator, as if they had veritable being. He was as interested in Harris' sons and in the entire family. . . . "All the between-whiles I've been 'sociatin' with you and 'Sister Jane'; and I must say it's mighty good company I've been in!"

The Book of Joyous Children was illustrated by Will

247

Vawter, as had been the *Child-Rhymes* and the *Farm-Rhymes,* and the artist's work did much to enhance the attractiveness of these volumes. Will Vawter was a native of Virginia, but had been reared in Greenfield; he knew Riley, he knew the Hoosier scene; he was adept at catching the spirit of the poems. Other men would illustrate other of Riley's books, but none so well as Vawter. . . .

Thereafter, Riley wrote less and less, dividing his waking hours between Lockerbie Street and the offices of his publishers or a downtown Indianapolis bookshop where he could be sure of meeting a few friends with whom to chat or exchange anecdotes. Immaculate and dapper, he was often to be glimpsed on Washington Street or pacing around the Circle, a distinguished pedestrian in his excellently cut, conservative clothes, his gray gloves, his eyeglasses with the satiny black ribbon.

He would be pointed out, whispered about. "There he is! There's Riley!" He did not object to that. He was fifty, and more, and did not look it. Nor did he admit it, either, always hedging a bit when asked how old he was, never telling precisely the truth.

Shepherded by solicitous teachers, schoolchildren flocked to see him in Lockerbie Street. Though he never turned them away, and was patient and even indulgent with them, showing them his white cat, his curly-haired and temperamental little poodle dog, he often was wearied by their shrill prattle and superabundant vitality. Children in the abstract, the child he had been, those in his memories, his brothers and sisters, Noey Bixler, Almon Keefer and Elmer Brown—they were less exhausting, dearer perhaps, than were the boys and girls hanging over his chair, rumpling him, breathing down his neck, plying him with queries. Yet he knew what his tact would mean to them—and to him. He was a hero and must not falter in the role; he was unfailingly courteous.

He liked better those evenings when he could converse and laugh with adult comrades; best of all, he liked the moments of solitude, in the safe haven of his room, the world shut out.

He clung to his friends and was merry with them; but beneath his sweetness and affability lay a streak of melancholy. He was always rather lonely.

He was constantly besieged by requests from young writers for advice and encouragement which he never refused. Meredith Nicholson, Booth Tarkington, Bliss Carman had been his protégés, as well as many others who, unlike these three, would never vindicate their early promise. Riley's custom, when a manuscript was sent to him, was to read it and then dash off across the top of the page one word, *"Fine!"* in bold pen strokes.

"The beginner thinks it's fine," he would say, "or he wouldn't have asked my opinion. And maybe it is!"

Remembering what encouragement had been to him, he could not bear to withhold it; and, also, he thought, these first flights might actually incorporate the spark of genius which a harsh or unappreciative criticism might extinguish. Where, he mused, would James Whitcomb Riley have been today, had not Longfellow been generous with him?

He conducted an extensive correspondence with friends in every section of the continent and in England, where his work was much esteemed. His letters were gay, blithe, charming—or they were tender, tinged with pathos. To the gay ones he signed himself as "Jamesy," or "James Popcorn Riley," or "James Whipcord Riley," or "James Hoosier Riley, the Whitcomb Poet." At other times he was "Ben Jamesie Schuffleberger," or something as grotesque. And in any letter, the expression of whatever mood, he was likely to insert some phrase of his sunny philosophy, his faith in God's goodness.

The years were lavish with their tokens.

In 1902, Riley was awarded the honorary degree of Master of Arts by Yale University, the suggestion for the decoration having originated with William Lyon Phelps, then Professor of American Literature at Yale. In 1903 Wabash College conferred upon him the Master of Arts degree. In 1904 the University of Pennsylvania gave him the degree of Doctor of Letters, never before bestowed upon a westerner. In 1907 Indiana University in a colorful ceremony made him an honorary Doctor of Letters.

Having so little formal education, Riley may have overvalued these academic laurels. But what man would not have been flattered, walking in the solemn processions, clothed in the mortarboard, the stole and hooded gown? His pride was not obvious or arrogant, but something deeply felt, a gentle humility.

In 1910 the Indiana Federation of Women's Clubs, acting upon the proposal of Mrs. Minnie Belle Mitchell of Greenfield, voted to celebrate Riley's birthday; the next year the school authorities directed teachers and pupils to observe October 7 as Riley Day. In the midst of congratulatory messages sent the poet from neighboring states and from Canada was one from the Bureau of Libraries in New York saying that 500,000 school-children of that state also would observe Riley Day.

In 1912 he was elected to the American Academy of Arts and Letters and awarded the gold medal for poetry. In June of the same year Anderson presented him with the keys to the city.

He went in his automobile to Anderson; all along the road farmers and their families had gathered to see him pass. Eight miles out from the town a huge delegation of cars and floats waited to escort him. Before the courthouse was a throng so clamorous and impenetrable that Riley must detour around it, while children rushed from all sides to throw flowers at him, to cover him, his party, and his chauffeur with a blanket of blossoms. When his automobile stopped, it was quickly netted over with chains of fragrant red clover, plucked from the meadows he had known so well in youth. The ovation lasted until dusk, with no slackening.

With such homage it must have seemed to him that he approached a climax. And so he did. He reached it in 1915, with a proclamation from the Governor of Indiana, the only one of its sort in the annals of literature.

". . . More than any other citizen of Indiana, James Whitcomb Riley has carried the fame of his native state into the schools and homes of the world. It is not strange therefore that there should be a widespread feeling among our people that the anniversary of his birth should be celebrated in honor of his poetic genius and his literary achievements, and in recognition of his contributions to society.

"He is the children's poet . . . All Indiana will rejoice therefore to see her children afforded an opportunity to place their heart wreaths upon his brow and strew their flowers at his feet.

"Now, therefore, I, Samuel M. Ralston, as Governor of the State of Indiana, hereby designate and proclaim the seventh day of October, A. D. 1915, the anniversary of the birth of James Whitcomb Riley as Riley Day; and I urge all the people of the state to arrange in their respective communities in their own way, appropriate exercises in their schools and at their other public meeting places; and that they display the American flag at their homes and places of business on this day, in honor of Indiana's most beloved citizen.

"IN WITNESS THEREOF, I have set my hand and caused to be affixed the Great Seal of the State of Indiana, at the Capitol, in the City of Indianapolis, this 8th day of September, A. D. 1915.

SAMUEL M. RALSTON,

GOVERNOR."

There was more to it than that, considerably more. Information soon arrived that the National Commissioner of Education had ordered that the seventh of October be celebrated in *all* the schools, private, public and parochial, of the United States.

Bouquets, gifts, telegrams, cablegrams flooded into Lockerbie in a mighty tide. Every instant of that day brought felicitations—from Woodrow Wilson, President of the United States, from William Dean Howells, Henry Watterson, Walt Mason, and a legion of friends and zealous champions in this country; from Walter Hines Page in London, Brand Whitlock in Belgium, Henry Van Dyke in The Netherlands.

Festivities culminated in a mammoth banquet in what has since been called the Riley Room of the Claypool Hotel in Indianapolis, with a program which included as speakers Governor Ralston, Senator John W. Kern, Albert J. Beveridge, William Allen White, George Ade. Charles Warren Fairbanks, formerly Vice-President, was the able toastmaster.

It was an evening with a crescendo of enthusiasm and expectancy. As the speeches ended, Senator Kern presented to the poet a silk flag, made for him and for the event, the offering of the Union Soldiers of Indiana.

253

When Riley got to his feet, the crowd rose with him, crying his name:

"James Whitcomb Riley. *Jim!*"

He was trembling. He thought he could not control his voice. But then, as always happened when he faced an audience, he looked about and was not frightened. These were his people, loving him as he loved them.

Slowly he said a few brave sentences of gratitude, to the President, and Mr. Howells, the distant friends who had sent greetings.

"—To him, to these, to all of *you*—I thank you." He paused. "And, in the words of little Tim Cratchit, 'God bless us every one'."

It was a wonderful moment, the most wonderful in the greatest day of his life.

He had been ailing for a long time, his health declining, sharply of late. But after the banquet he was stronger. He went south for a winter in Florida, and came back to the Indiana spring. He was happy, hopeful for recovery. But on the night of July 22, 1916, he fell asleep—and did not waken.

With dawn the news filtered from Lockerbie Street, over the city, along the National Pike where stood the substantial white frame dwelling, into Greenfield. By noon the nation had heard. The Hoosier Poet had gone, never to return.

254

Hoosier Poet

Millions of men and women grieved, children's eyes were misty with honest tears. From hearts and lips everywhere welled a murmuring, a phrase from one of his own verses, so simple, so infinitely sincere:

" 'Goodbye, Jim. Take keer of yourse'f.' "

Bibliography

The Complete Works of James Whitcomb Riley, Collected and edited by Edmund Henry Eitel. Biographical edition, six volumes. Indianapolis: the Bobbs-Merrill Co., 1913.

The Youth of James Whitcomb Riley, by Marcus Dickey. Indianapolis: the Bobbs-Merrill Co., 1919.

The Maturity of James Whitcomb Riley, by Marcus Dickey. Indianapolis: the Bobbs-Merrill Co., 1922.

Letters of James Whitcomb Riley, edited by William Lyon Phelps. Indianapolis: the Bobbs-Merrill Co., 1930.

James Whitcomb Riley, Reminiscences, by Clara E. Laughlin. New York, Chicago: Fleming H. Revell Co., 1930.

History of Hancock County, Indiana, by John C. Binford. Greenfield, Indiana: King and Binford, 1882.

History of Hancock County, Indiana, by George J. Richman. Greenfield, Indiana: William Mitchell Printing Co., 1916.

257

Bibliography

History of Indiana, by Logan Esary. Dayton Historical Publishing Co., 1922.

Greenfield, the Historic Birthplace of the Nation's Poet, by Minnie Belle Mitchell, Greenfield, Indiana. The Mitchell Co., 1925.

Indianapolis, the Old Town and the New, by Lee Burns. Indianapolis, 1923.

The Hoosiers, by Meredith Nicholson. New York: The Macmillan Co., 1900.

A Hoosier Chronicle, by Meredith Nicholson. Boston and New York: Houghton Mifflin Company, 1912.

The Poet, by Meredith Nicholson. Boston: Houghton Mifflin Co., 1914.

The Man in the Street, by Meredith Nicholson. New York: Charles Scribner's Sons, 1925.

Poets and Poetry of Indiana, by B. S. Parker and E. B. Heiney. Boston: Silver, Burdett and Co., 1900.

Poets of America, by Edmund Clarence Stedman. Boston and New York: Houghton Mifflin Co., 1885.

The Wabash, by William E. Wilson. New York: Farrar and Rinehart, 1940.

Studies in American and British Literature, by Inez N. McFee. Chicago: A. Flanagan Co., 1905.

The Children's Poets, by Walter Barnes. Yonkers-on-Hudson, New York: World Book Co., 1924.

Through Golden Windows, by Mary K. Reely and Ada Randall. Chicago: Whitman Co., 1935.

Worlds and I, by Ella Wheeler Wilcox. New York: George H. Doran Co., 1918.

Bibliography

ARTICLES IN PERIODICALS AND NEWSPAPERS

Atlantic Monthly, vol. lxxxii (1898): "Mr. Riley's Poetry," by Bliss Carman.

Book Buyer, vol. xvii (1898): "James Whitcomb Riley as a Poet of Childhood," by C. E. Laughlin.

Book News, vol. xxv (1907): "Riley — Poet of the People," by Bliss Carman.

"Christian Science Monitor," October 7, 1937: "Indiana Honors Memory of Hoosier Poet."

Delineator, vol. lxxii (1908): "In Lockerbie Street," by Mabel Potter Daggett.

Ladies' Home Journal, vol. xix (1902): "Riley's Home Folks," by J. F. Mitchell, Jr.

——— vol. xxxii (1915): "The Real Orphant Annie," by Edmund Eitel.

Harper's Monthly Magazine, vol. cxxvi (1917 and 1918): "The Letters of James Whitcomb Riley," Arranged with Comment, by Edmund H. Eitel.

Western Association of Writers: A Souvenir of the Fourth Annual Convention at Warsaw, Indiana, 1889.

——— *Proceedings of the Fifth Annual Convention at Eagle Lake, Indiana,* 1890.

Philadelphia *Bulletin* (August 5, 1937): "James Whitcomb Riley," by William Lyon Phelps.

ALSO

The files of the *Greenfield Democrat,* the *Greenfield Reporter,* and the *Greenfield Republican.*

The files of the *Indianapolis Journal,* the *Indianapolis News,* and the *Indianapolis Star.*

259

Bibliography

"Riley Loved Children," an address delivered by George C. Hitt, in Indianapolis, October 7, 1936.

"James Whitcomb Riley," an address delivered by Meredith Nicholson, Indianapolis, October 6, 1911.

"Riley Day," by Charles A. Greathouse; a booklet published at Indianapolis by the State Superintendent of Public Instruction, 1915.

Index

261

Index

Index

263

Index

265

ROBISON '41